TURNING THE WORLD RIGHT-SIDE UP

REFLECTIONS ON THE KINGDOM OF GOD AND THE BEATITUDES

NAVAZ DCRUZ

Someone said that if you want to leave a legacy, write.
So, I write for this generation and the ones yet to come.
This book is something the coming generations can read long after
I have finished my race and fought the fight of faith.

Contents

Foreword

A measure of a book can be evaluated by its un-putdown-ability. What do I mean? I'm coining or stretching the word "unputdownable" to make a point. Quite simply, that's what I felt when reading the soft copy of the manuscript that Navaz sent me. I felt frustrated each time the 'pressures' of time or my indiscipline prompted me to defer reading momentarily.

I discovered I could not *just* read or devour this spiritually alluring book. The Sermon on the Mount, which is what the book is based on, is a muscle-building, robust, balanced diet in itself. These rich, raw food words of Jesus, processed through a chef's contemplative, spirit-filled, trademark diligence, transform Jesus' health-giving words into tasty, sumptuous meals. The timeless becalming effect of the beatitudes, piling on mind-blowing, oxymoronic, counter-cultural blessings, e.g. "Blessed are the meek for they shall inherit the earth", for those who believe, are a sheer delight to the pallets of the gourmets of the spirit. Even Mahatma Gandhi couldn't resist reading portions of these profound thoughts at his public meetings.

Navaz has grown. Navaz has outshone herself. Each of Jesus' gripping thoughts has been broken down and processed through the prism of other scriptures and the touchstone of being lived out or at least an attempt to do so. The book's strength is that it is gospel-based. The high standards to be outlived are upheld by the enabling grace that comes through abiding in Jesus and not striving in one's legalistic self-efforts. The bibliography speaks of a fortification of doctrinal truth through sound teaching by reputed men and women of God. The teacher in Navaz is conspicuously evident. The chopped pieces are blended and cooked into a delicious book dish to follow the chef's analogy.

This book can't *just* be read. It needs meditation, discussion and application. Navaz, the pastoral practitioner has helpfully provided an Action Page at the end of each Beatitude that could help personal study or group discussion to bite, chew, consume and digest the spread before us. There's plenty for body, mind, emotions and spirit. And it's all about the wholeness that comes from walking radically with Jesus, its author and finisher.

This book was first written as a series of devotionals for the YOUVERSION Bible App. This would be a longer version of the same. Give thanks and eat, for "blessed are those who hunger and thirst for righteousness, for they shall be filled (Matt 5:6)"

David Fernandes.
Pastor Emeritus and Mentor-Coach

Endoresement

Join the crowds and sit at Jesus' feet as you engage in this comprehensive study of the Beatitudes. You'll smell the dust of the Galilean hillside, feel the hustle and bustle of the expectant crowd and hear the hushed moments as the authoritative voice of Jesus brought an understanding of His Kingdom. Navaz D'Cruz's in-depth study of this key passage will take you to that hillside, and you will find it life-giving and extremely inspiring.

The depth and layers of well-thought-through information used to contextualise the teaching are amazing. I love the tone and details. It is thought-provoking and very accessible.

I highly recommend this study of The Beatitudes. What a resource for Christian living!

Steve Oliver

Founder of Regions Beyond

Some books inform us, books that inspire us, and then there are books that quietly but firmly reorient our lives. Turning the World Right Side Up by Navaz D'Cruz belongs to the latter category. From the first page, it is clear that this is not merely a book to be read, but an invitation to be transformed.

One line in particular stayed with me: "What is hidden in the roots will be revealed in the shoots." These words capture the heart of this book. Navaz reminds us that what we cultivate within—our loves, convictions, and understanding of God's Kingdom—will inevitably shape how we live and what we offer to the world. With courage and clarity, she weaves together deep theology and practical discipleship, calling readers to a faith that is both rooted and active.

Beginning with the Kingdom of God, Navaz establishes a strong biblical foundation and gently confronts an essential question: do we begin our spiritual journey with ourselves, or with God? As the book unfolds, the gospel is presented with clarity and conviction.

Particularly striking is the way Navaz holds together Reformed theology, a missional vision, and charismatic vitality. This integration reflects not only theological depth but a lived passion for the things of God.

A key strength of this book is its ability to shift our focus from what feels urgent to what is eternally important. By drawing us back to the Beatitudes and the Sermon on the Mount, Navaz reminds us that life in God's Kingdom requires direction. Without it, we are like travellers without a compass. With it, we learn to seek first what truly matters.

Designed with reflection and action in mind, this book serves as an excellent companion for personal growth and discipleship. Wherever you find yourself on your journey, I believe Turning the World Right Side Up will challenge you, encourage you, and invite you to live more fully rooted in the Kingdom of God.

Vinu Paul
Leader of Commission, an apostolic sphere within
Newfrontiers and lead pastor of Living Faith Church.

"To grasp the true meaning of the Beatitudes, one must first understand the vital concept of the Kingdom of God. In this book, Navaz combines in-depth theological insight, an accessible writing style, and real-life examples to lay a strong foundation that challenges our thinking and fuels our mission."

Dr.Joshua George
Academic Dean - SAIACS

Acknowledgements

Writing this book has not been easy, as I was writing during a season of many changes in our lives involving many twists and turns. I want to acknowledge Colin, my husband, for standing with me, celebrating who I am, and making the space for me to flourish.

A big thank you to the rest of the family and friends who have always encouraged me to keep writing.

Thank you, *David Fernandes,* who has always championed me, and once again, be gracious enough to write the Forward for this my second book (a hat-trick probably awaits!). Thank you, *Steve Oliver,* who sent me such encouraging texts and voice notes to urge me on to the finish line. Thank you, *Dr. Joshua George,* my dear friend, who gave me constructive feedback and urged me not to give up. Thank you, *Daniel Mcleod,* for taking the trouble to read the draft and coming back with so many positive and helpful suggestions. Thank you, *Usha Srinivasan,*for being such a helpful sounding board. A special thank you to *Jessica,* our daughter, who has painstakingly read and re-read my drafts.

Thank *Jesus* that you do not give up on me and that your grace invites me to bear a yoke that is easy. You made a way for us to be truly human.

Navaz D'Cruz
Oct 2024

Preface

After I wrote my first book, I faced some of the greatest challenges in loving people. I began to wonder what it must look like to be truly human, like how it was supposed to be in an uncorrupted Eden. God always longed for peculiar people who would demonstrate His image-bearing qualities in how they lived. I felt the Holy Spirit guide me in studying the Beatitudes, and I thought to myself, 'Ah! What better place to get my head, heart, and hands sorted than here?'

As I read and meditated on these scriptures, I realized that my thoughts, heart, and behaviour were far from the truth. I noticed how compromised they had become with what everyone quickly excuses as 'being human'! So often, I got angry and harboured vengeful prayers as I read the news about all the injustices happening in my country and worldwide. This provoked me to think of the old saying, ' What would Jesus do?'

During this season, we also went through some challenging times as a church community, and this scripture passage put my heart to the test. How do I be meek when the urge is to give a harsh retort? How do I show mercy when all I want to do is call out their wrong? The challenge to maintain a pure heart when it would have been easier to manipulate tested me in a secret place where no one could see what was going in my heart.

I realized that if I were not careful, I would slowly get cooked in a pot, thus compromising with culture; I would lose my saltiness and cease to be the light Jesus had asked me to be. Thus began my journey of studying the Beatitudes, which became a sermon series we did at our church, then a YouVersion devotional and now a book.

I am still on this journey as I turn my life around to align with the Beatitudes. I know this process will continue until He returns or calls me home. So, in the words of Paul *"Not that I have already obtained all this, or have already arrived at my goal, but I press on to take hold of that for which Christ Jesus took hold of me"* (Phil

3:12). I echo the same thought. I do not write as one who has arrived; rather, I share revelations that challenge my heart daily toward renewal and repentance. I invite you to walk with me on that journey of growth.

- Navaz D Cruz

Oct 2024

Introduction

I am deeply amazed by how God has guided me, His image bearer, deeper into His heart. He has been revealing His profound love for humanity to me. I realized that if I do not truly grasp Jesus's love, I might misconstrue His teachings as mere rules and regulations. Through the Sermon on the Mount, He showed how the Law needed to be applied.

Throughout Biblical history, the Israelites took His law and misinterpreted it, making it cold and calculating. When Jesus came, He ushered in His Kingdom, showing us how His law needs to be understood. Where the Ten Commandments started with many dos and don'ts, the Beatitudes begin with "Blessed are", and show us how we ought to *be* instead.

Jesus' focus has always been on our relationship with Him. He was interested in the heart of the matter, and that is why He challenged the status quo. Jesus starts His ministry by announcing, 'Repent, for the Kingdom of God is at hand,' and goes on to show how it ought to be lived by a correct application of His law.

When God created the world, He created humanity to co-exist with Him. Psalm 8 also reflects this intent of God when the Psalmist says, '*You have made them a little lower than the angels and crowned them with glory and honour. You made them rulers over the works of your hands; you put everything under their feet.*' God put two trees in the garden. His purpose was for Adam and Eve to rely on Him for guidance rather than trying to pursue the understanding of the knowledge of good and evil independent of Him. By pursuing a path apart from God, they were led away from the wisdom that is pure and peaceable, that originates in the heart of God.

Apart from God, our understanding of good and evil gets distorted because it is defined by an evil being, Satan - the father of lies. He will get us to believe that good is evil and vice versa or sell us dangerous half-truths, if not worse. Isn't that why the world is so messed up in their understanding of right and wrong? Perfect wisdom and truth can only be found in God.

However, as we know, the story did not end there. God set in motion a plan to re-establish His Kingdom and reassert His rule over the kingdoms of this world. The Sermon on the Mount describes the kingdom's lifestyle and values. It expands on the two greatest commands: *love God and love your neighbour as yourself.* Jesus expects us to love ourselves the same way He loves us, which is complete and unconditional. Only when we mirror Jesus' love by embracing it in our lives can we authentically share it with others.

As I ponder upon all this, I realise I am wading ankle-deep into His purpose and design for us, those He calls the Light of the World. Only when I draw closer to The *Light of the World* can I reflect His light in and through my life. We must draw closer to Him and go deeper into His presence from ankle to waist, to shoulder deep until we are fully in over our heads of His presence. As we do this, we will become that catalyst of change that brings life and light into the world. We will become that life-giving tree planted by the ever-flowing stream of the Holy Spirit's enabling power to heal the nations He always intended.

While writing this book, I noticed myself repeating key concepts. I became acutely aware of how intricately layered in width and depth Jewish thought is, contrary to the Western/ Greek linear learning style. So, as I see the connections, I re-echo these concepts so that you, too, can see how they are all interconnected.

Before we dive into the Beatitudes, it is important to understand what the Kingdom of God is like because The Beatitudes must be understood in that context. Also, studying the entire Sermon on the Mount would be a great exercise (Matthew chapters five through seven), but I have decided to focus on just the Beatitudes in this book. Perhaps part two will reflect on the rest of the Sermon on the Mount. But for now, may I invite you to journey with me as we explore one of the most profound themes woven into scripture from Genesis chapter One to Revelation twenty-two.

HOW TO READ THIS BOOK

I wrote this book to inspire reflection and heart transformation, echoing Jesus' call for us to 'repent' and turn from our old ways. The danger of overfamiliarity with popular scripture passages is the assumption that we practice them because we know. Overfamiliarity can close us off to fresh revelations that the Holy Spirit gives us. As John Stott said, *"The Sermon on the Mount is the best known, least understood, and least obeyed."*

Here is how you can read this book:

- Read the whole book to get a wide understanding of Jesus' teaching.
- Then read it slowly, chapter by chapter, to go deeper. Allow the Holy Spirit to speak to you and turn things around in your heart.
- Go over the **Key Turning Points** to help summarise the main thoughts for each Beatitude.
- Ponder the questions in the **Reflections** section, as we do not merely want to hear the Word obey it.
- Use the **Notes** section to jot down any revelations, convictions, and actions you will put into practice. I call it the 'Head, Heart, and Hands' section. It allows you to journal your thoughts and what the Holy Spirit makes you aware of.

You could also use this book to study in small groups. More than anything, I pray that your heart is challenged daily, as mine is.

PART 1 - THE KINGDOM OF GOD

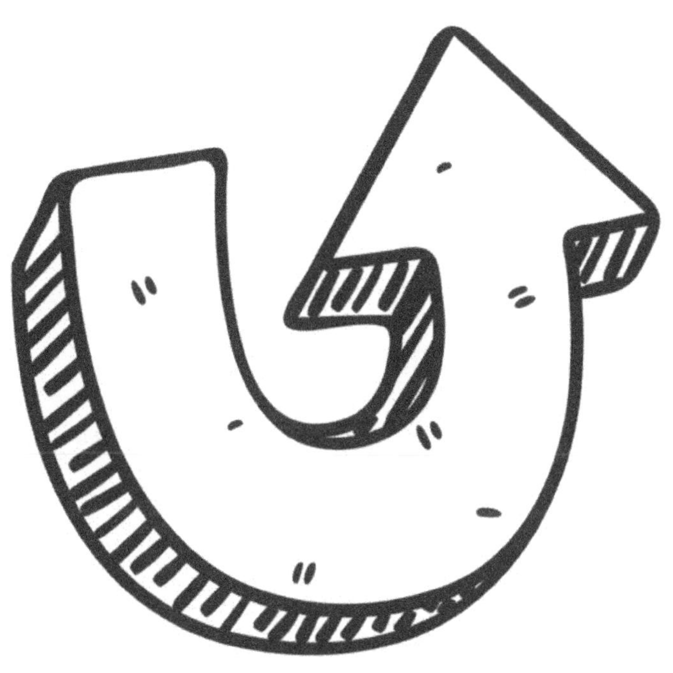

CHAPTER I

THE DELIVERER

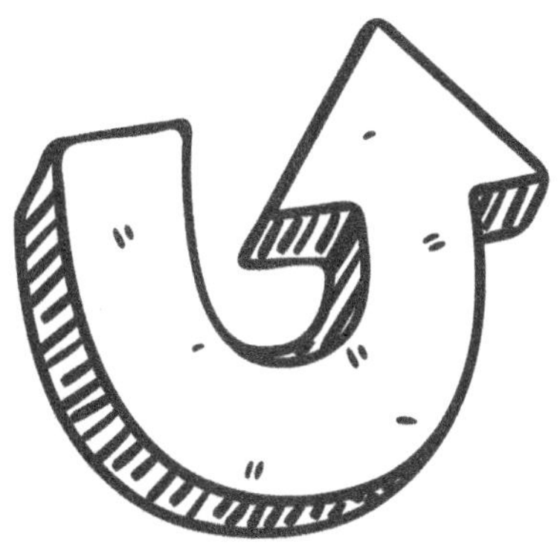

Amid a cacophony of chatter, many voices posed as wisdom with instructions to tame the sinful human heart into rigid, penitentiary conformity. But there was silence from the One voice that mattered the most! A silence that lasted four centuries. That voice that had the power to speak life into everything fell silent.

A people peculiar in nature but corrupt in heart and hand still longingly waited for that very voice to speak. They knew it could break bondages and shatter shackles, just as they had so often heard read from the scrolls every sabbath within the hallowed walls of the synagogue. The same people who, when enslaved in a foreign land, cried for a deliverer thousands of years ago, now echo that cry again: "When will the Deliverer come?"

However, in the fullness of time, what may have seemed to happen suddenly, was an unusual phenomenon that filled the night sky. Heaven's silence was finally broken with a loud and lusty cry from a child born in obscurity in an overcrowded city during a census. Indeed, many babies were born that night, yet magnificent, winged celestial creatures left their heavenly realms and descended into Earth's atmosphere to announce only one birth.

Lowly shepherds viewed by society as thieving vagabonds and, therefore, unreliable witnesses were the chosen human heralds, indicating that nothing about the events that would unfold from here on would be 'usual'.

Chaos would ensue before any order could be restored. Things that got turned upside down because of one self-willed, selfish act in a garden will now get turned the right side up by one selfless act of surrender. This would happen in a garden once again and by a sacrifice on a redeeming tree!

The first image bearer lost his identity and authority to reign over Earth as he succumbed to the temptation to self-rule rather than rule under God's authority. He sold his birthright for a bite of the forbidden fruit. Meanwhile, the deliverer who was to come would sip the cup of suffering for the sins of the fallen world.

Now, the divine takes the form of one He created to show Image Bearer how to do things correctly. The incarnation of God into humanity had to take place to show us how to be human as God originally intended.

For thirty years, the character of the Creator was crafted in a carpenter's shop. In a dusty work shed and under the watchful father's eye, before any of His public life could begin, the young apprentice learned in quietness and obedience from the very ones He created. His earthly parents humbly and reverently undertook this responsibility of stewarding the Lord of History, neither fully knowing nor understanding but just living by faith.

The time finally came! Dusty roads, milling crowds, all yearning for deliverance from brutal oppression, and abject poverty filled the road toward the river. A voice cried aloud in the wilderness, beckoning people to repentance and spiritual cleansing. Was He 'the One'? He sure sounded like it, but he was dressed differently and looked strange!

Then, sandal-shorn feet walked up the well-worn path, dust clouds filling the air as people jostled against each other, pushing forward impatiently for their turn for a baptism of repentance. As the splashes of water quieten and the next one gets into the water, John sees feet approach him. He gazes not into the face of a cousin but the Creator of all, the 'one' everyone longed for and for whom he was just the way maker. Unable to restrain himself, he cries, 'Behold the Lamb of God who takes away the sins of the World!'.

A new, much-awaited Kingdom is about to be ushered in, part of one big, unified story. This is a Kingdom that does not have a beginning or an end; it has always been. The King Himself, who stepped down from the heights of heaven, came to earth to teach His new subjects how to live as citizens of this new Kingdom, which He often said was 'not of this world'. He was going to turn everything they knew on its head and shed His light on their understanding and in their hearts. And He started on a hillside, taking the posture of a Rabbi, sat down and began to teach His newly acquired subjects, opening His discourse with, "Blessed are." Now, history would never be the same!

CHAPTER II

THE KINGDOM OF GOD

The deliverer, the long-awaited Messiah and King of the Jews had indeed stepped down from His throne to dwell amongst His created beings. He was on a mission to bring the Kingdom of God here on earth as it is in heaven. Understanding the background and context is essential before diving into the Beatitudes. "The Kingdom" is a theme that runs through the Bible. Without understanding the Kingdom of God, it will be challenging to fully appreciate what Jesus was saying and connect the dots between the Kingdom of God, the Beatitudes, the entire Sermon on the Mount and the Law. So, in the following four chapters, we will examine the nature of the Kingdom of God. Here we go!

GOD AND HIS KINGDOM THROUGH SCRIPTURE

Right from the time of creation, the ancient world has seen many watershed events that are markers in history; there is Creation, the Fall, the flood, the Tower of Babel (the Bronze and Iron Ages), the Egyptian empire, the Red Sea Crossing, the covenants given to Moses and the birth of the nation Israel, the kings of Israel, the rise of the Babylonian empire, the fall of Jerusalem, the period of captivity and exile, the return from exile, the rise of the Greek and Roman empires, and finally the 400 years of silence at the end of the Old Testament era.

Through the ages, God has always been King Eternal. His Kingdom did not start with the creation of the world. He ruled unchallenged from a place of timelessness into and through time. Then Lucifer challenged His kingship and thought he could be an equal, if not a better rival, to God. How mistaken! God hurled him into the darkness with nothing and into nothingness—dark and void (Gen 1:2).

LIGHT AND THE KINGDOM

Then God created the Earth to become a place of light and life (Gen1:3). It is interesting to note that the first thing God commands into being on Earth is light! Noticing this, I see a stream of light shining throughout scripture. God describes Himself as light and dwelling in unapproachable light (1 Tim 6:16). We live under the two great lights, one in the day and one at night, that God created to be a constant reminder that He is *the* Great Light of the World.

Isaiah prophesied the coming Messiah by proclaiming, "Arise, and shine, your light has come." (Is. 60:1). The Gospel of John starts by calling the Word who becomes flesh, The Light of all humanity (John 1:4, 8-9). Jesus refers to Himself as the Light of the World (John 8:12) and calls us the world's light (Matt 5:14-16)! Can you imagine that? We are Light; this is one of the first things Jesus tells

His followers about who they are. The Kingdom's mandate is for us to be Light to the nations.

Our intimacy with Jesus is compared to lamps that burn brightly and do not run out of oil (Matt 25:1-13). This theme is carried on in the epistles, where we are asked to let our light shine through our good deeds so that the glory goes to God. All this culminates with Jesus' glorious return with trumpets shattering the sound barrier between heaven and earth and our Lord descending through the clouds to take us back with Him to Heaven (1 Thes 4:16-17) where there is neither sun nor moon and the Lamb will be its light.

CREATION AND THE KINGDOM

Coming back to creation, God speaks words that breathe life. He breaks the silence with His voice. He brings forth heavenly bodies and makes the earth a thing of astounding beauty and splendour, endowed with landscapes only a genius God could come up with. The world is now teeming with all kinds of creatures on land, in the sky and sea, all in a kaleidoscope of colours, shapes and form.

And then – finally, God creates and fashions His Image Bearer, not with His voice but lovingly with His hands and kiss of life. This image bearer is a blend of the earth (dust) and the divine (the breath of God), a combination that no other creature has. That is why only humans are called Image Bearers. His image bearers reflect His kingly likeness and divine qualities of giving life. No wonder God commanded man not to make any graven 'images' of Him. He has already displayed His image and glory in humans. Anything else would fall short and misrepresent God. God gave His Image Bearer the authority to rule and have dominion over everything, including Lucifer. This authority was granted, provided the image bearer continued to live in obedience and dependence on God for the knowledge and wisdom to govern everything. This kingdom's theme of rulership is seen right at the start of creation.

Now, the Image Bearers took matters into their own hands the day they decided to get knowledge apart from God by eating from the forbidden tree. You see, what they did not know was that without God, they would lose their moral compass because only God, who is The Truth, knows what is truly good and evil. Our perception of truth gets distorted outside of His presence and influence. Adam and Eve's disobedience was costly. They forfeited the right to be under God's kingdom when they sinned. Not only that, but they also gave up the privilege and right to reign and rule the earth. They handed that reign over to Satan and became subject to his cruel rule and to his kingdom of darkness, where God's light is absent because God's presence cannot dwell in sin.

However, God always wanted a people for Himself, a people peculiar, princely and priestly set apart for Himself. He chose Abraham, from whom a vast nation was born, just like He had promised. Then, as history unfolds, God's people land in Egypt during the famine, where Joseph saves the people of Israel from famine. However, in time, they became enslaved in Egypt for 400 long years. God sent a deliverer in Moses to take them to the Promised Land, where they would finally be His people, and He would be their God. This event is but a shadow of another event that was preceded by 400 years of silence before the true Deliverer came to set His people free. They walked through the Red Sea victorious. But having been enslaved for so long, they did not know how to relate with God even though He demonstrated His love for them in such might through signs and wonders. They did not know how to reign and live as free people because all they knew was enslavement.

Instead of relating to God face-to-face, they preferred a graven image mediator of the golden calf. When God called them up to the mountain to meet Him, they responded in fear and preferred to interact with Him through rules and regulations. Thus, were born the Ten Commandments and another 600 laws they were to live by. Even in this, one could see the Kingdom of God. If only they could see and understand it through the right lens. But it took a few thousand years for the right time for all things to be revealed through Jesus.

A NEW ERA - THE KINGDOM HERE ON EARTH AS IT IS IN HEAVEN

Then, a new era burst upon the scene not with fanfare but in humble obscurity in a cowshed, witnessed by animals and lowly shepherds. A New Era was born that night, and heaven would not keep silent but rushed towards earth to sing "Glory in the highest and peace on earth".

The King of the universe stepped down from the heights of heaven into darkness and sinful humanity. This event was cataclysmic and had a significant bearing on human history. The world was reeling under oppressive rules from Kingdoms and religious systems that opposed the Creator's Kingdom. From Adam's fall, these two Kingdoms were at war.

THE CROSS AND THE KINGDOM

God's salvation plan was coming to a culmination and coming into play. The Messiah was born. He was going to usher in a kingdom unlike any other, where the humble would be exalted, the servant of all would be the greatest of all, and the one who denies his life would gain it.

Jesus started His ministry by saying, "Repent for the Kingdom of God has come". He taught His disciples to pray, "Your kingdom come here on earth as it is in heaven". In the Sermon on the Mount, Jesus explains what His kingdom looks like and how its subjects ought to behave. It countered anything they had heard before. Where the Jews sought a physical revolution that they would fight for by striking their enemy with a sword, Jesus taught them to offer the other cheek when struck, to walk the extra mile, to give their cloak to anyone who asks, and to be the first to forgive. He challenged us to bless those who persecute us and pray for those who despitefully use us and who might even kill us. He knew His preaching would be tested in His life by a betrayal for thirty pieces of silver and a denial thrice over. Jesus was creating a culture where heart transformation is at its core. He wanted to make a body of disciples who would be apostolic, and they would influence the culture by how they lived.

The Kingdom comes into an even fuller view on the day of Pentecost when the church is born and becomes the empowered agent and vehicle to take God's kingdom to the ends of the earth. As salt and light, the church is scattered and dispersed throughout the known world and to the regions beyond.

Jesus had given His disciples the authority to open new doors, ushering in God's reign and rule. What Jesus did was the beginning of the fulfilment of Habakkuk's prophecy of the Earth being filled with the knowledge and the glory of the Lord even as the waters cover the sea (Hab 2:14)

We can see Ezekiel's vision (Ezek. 47) of the river flowing out from the temple and growing deeper and broader, coming to pass as the church (the new temple where God dwells) going out from the presence of God carrying His life-giving mandate everywhere. We finally end up in the book of Revelation, which talks at length about the Kingdom of God, where people from every nation, tribe and tongue will gather before the great white throne on which the Lamb of God will be seated (Rev 11:15, Rev 7:11-17). Everything comes full circle with the Tree of Life that is in heaven for the healing of the nations (Rev 22:1-5), and we will reign with Jesus forever!

JESUS AND THE KINGDOM

Jesus starts His ministry while John the Baptist is in prison, picking up where he left off with the same clarion call: "Repent, for the Kingdom of God is near" (Matt 4:17). He heals the sick, casts out demons, and preaches about the Kingdom of God. He became famous throughout Syria, Decapolis, Judea, Jerusalem, and Jordan. This was quite a large region (approximately 200,000 square kilometres) in the ancient world, especially where people mainly travelled on foot. Only the wealthy could afford horses or perhaps a donkey. News was delivered through word of mouth or by hand-delivered letters. During these times, Jesus had gathered a substantial following and became quite influential.

REPENT

"Repent, for the kingdom of heaven has come near." (Matt 4:17). What a strange way to announce one's Kingdom or ministry! This was

far from what the Jews expected their Messiah to say. Why was Jesus calling for repentance? What kind of repentance is He calling people to? John the Baptist was already calling people to repentance for sins, as we see in Matthew 3:2: *"Repent, for the kingdom of heaven has come near'"* Here is the difference: when John called for repentance from sinful deeds, Jesus is now calling for repentance from wrong beliefs and thinking that was reflected in the way they lived.

"Repent" as John the Baptist used the term, is not just an expression of sorrow over sin. More importantly, it also meant a change of mind, heart, and, therefore, actions. Jesus is drawing their attention to thinking in a new way. The Greek word used is *metanoeite*. Paul uses the same root word when he writes about being transformed by renewing our minds in the book of Romans.

""Repentance, therefore, is not only the only way into the Kingdom, but it is also the way of the Kingdom."
Christopher Morgan.""

Consequently, I am challenged to change my thinking through the daily process of repentance. There is so much that needs to be renewed and un-squeezed from the world's mould so that I can reflect Kingdom culture rather than the world's culture.

THE KINGDOM OF HEAVEN

The book of Matthew refers to the Kingdom more than fifty times. Jesus spoke a lot about the Kingdom of God. The word 'Kingdom' is mentioned 162 times in the New Testament and 126 times in the gospels alone in the context of the 'Kingdom of God/Heaven'.

What does the word 'Kingdom' mean? The English word refers to a place. The Greek, *Basileia*, and Hebrew *Malkuth* refer to an activity of action. The Latin word is 'Dom', which means power, authority, and dominion. From this word, we get the English words freedom, stardom, martyrdom, etc.

The Biblical or Jewish understanding refers to it as an action of rulership or to reign. So, to reference the 'reign' of the King is the same as saying the "Kingdom" of a King".[i]

We tend to visualise "Kingdom" as a geographical space defined by borders, but the biblical understanding is an activity so a better translation would have been "*reign*" When we relook at what Jesus said, "Repent, for the *reign* of God is near", we can understand it differently. It means the ruling activity of a king. Jesus is announcing the arrival of God's reign on earth, a Kingdom that transcends geography and borders of any kind.

Adam, as we saw earlier, forfeited his authority and ability to reign when he listened to Satan. Walking in obedience to God was the key to Adam's authority. He handed that key over to Satan when he and Eve disobeyed God's command. In the same way, now, the keys of the Kingdom unlock God's reign when it is outworked in an obedient, surrendered life, just as a key must surrender itself to the confines of a keyhole. Only Jesus, the obedient Adam and Son of God could take back what the first Adam handed over to Satan.

Jesus' Kingdom transcends time and space because He did not come to establish an earthly kingdom; rather, He was about to bring His kingdom *reign* here on earth, as it is in heaven.

The Jews sought a Messiah King who would usher in a Kingdom. And this is what He says, "You want to be included in the Kingdom of heaven? Then be poor in Spirit!"

FROM HILL TO HILL, FROM LAW TO LOVE.

Jesus gave His New Covenant commandments sitting on the top of a hill. Thousands of years earlier, God gave the Ten Commandments to the Israelites at Mount Sinai for their good and to keep them from harm. However, those commands became cold rules that were harshly used to punish lawbreakers. Here, Jesus invites people to draw close to Him. He did not teach from any particular mountain like Mount Zion but from an ordinary one, showing that sacred spaces were no longer in places but in the person of the Messiah. I am reminded of Jesus' discourse with the woman at the well when she talks about worshipping at this mountain and that. Jesus' response foretells what was to come: people from every race, tribe and tongue could worship Him from anywhere, for the Father is looking for worshippers who will worship in Spirit and in Truth. What a turning point.

I have also been thinking: How did David love the law of the Lord so much that he wrote so many beautiful psalms about it? The longest one, Psalm 119, is a tribute to the Law of God. That makes me think—it could not have been so awful! What was truly terrible was its interpretation and practice.

Jesus is the Word of God and, therefore, the law of God. Is He bad? It is like someone using a Ferrari as a wagon to be pulled by two bulls, complaining that the "cart" is so cumbersome and useless. It is a complete misuse and abuse of a beautiful car until the carmaker comes along and shows you how to use it. He untethers the vehicle from the bulls and shows the people how it was meant to be used.

Jesus shows us the Way, the Truth, and the Life and sheds light on how these laws must be understood and applied. The Sermon on the Mount is an exegesis or explanation of the Torah, showing people the real heart behind the Law, which was always about relationship and love. Reflecting on this, I realise that apart from a relationship with God, I will never understand the heart behind His Word, and I could be in danger of missing the point.

THE SERMON

Matthew 5:1 says Jesus sat down and began to teach. His sitting down meant He took the position of a Rabbi. Luke 6:17 records an incident where Jesus stood and preached at a *"level place"*. Scholars say that Jesus often preached the same message in different places and towns He visited. That is why you might notice slight variations of the same sermon. Matthew records the most extended version of this sermon, where Jesus compares His teaching to the Torah, saying, *"You have heard it said, but I say to you"* (Matt 5:21-33). The Jews, unlike us, were aware of the original text to which Jesus was referring. They could see the sharp contrast in their understanding and application of the texts Jesus quoted. Some of them perhaps were beginning to see how Jesus' challenge to *"repent"* differed from John the Baptist's. Luke's version, however, is shorter and does not have a comparison with the Torah, as his audience was not Jewish. Here, we can also see the seeds of the early church taking root in these first gatherings of disciples.

CLASH OF THE KINGDOMS

We know Jesus came to usher in a kingdom unlike any other. It was a counter-culture kingdom. We need to understand what the word Kingdom meant to the original readers who are Jewish with a Jewish understanding but also Jews who are living under Roman occupation, culture, and rule. In those days, anyone who challenged Caesar, who was considered Kristos, or the Lord and Saviour of the people, could be killed. So, you can immediately see how Jesus is disrupting their thought and understanding and showing them where their true allegiance ought to lie and who was the true Saviour. We see a clash of two spiritual kingdoms and a worldly kingdom governed by a dark spiritual kingdom opposed to God. This contrast between the Kingdom of Jesus and the Roman rule is not just a historical fact, but a tension that underscores the radical nature of Jesus' message.

I reflect and re-look at how Paul talks of the kingdom and what he must have been alluding to when he wrote Philippians 2, where he talks of Jesus, who has the *"Name above every other name"* and yet a sharp contrast to earthly kings and rulers. These were terms reserved for the Emperor of Rome alone.

Is the Kingdom of God a New Testament concept? The Kingdom of God is an eternal concept that existed before time began. Jesus prayed, *"Your Kingdom come'"* However, in the Old Testament, the people wanted an earthly King. The prophets and the psalmist speak of God's Kingdom viz—the Psalms, and in the book of Daniel. The Jews longed for a Messiah to come as a Saviour who would also be a conquering King who would overthrow Rome. However, Jesus comes as a King, laying aside His majesty and divinity. He came as the Son of Man and a Servant King. So, let us look at the Kingdom of God with an open heart and fresh eyes and trust the Holy Spirit to realign us.

[i] Why is Jesus always talking about the Kingdom of God – Bible Project.

CHAPTER IV

CHARACTERISTICS OF THE KINGDOM OF GOD

BIBLICAL CONTEXT AND LANGUAGE

A diligent student of scripture will always strive to comprehend the passage they are reading within its historical and cultural context. The imagery, metaphors, and words in the Bible held vastly different meanings for the listeners of that time. As N.T. Wright aptly puts it, the Bible was not written *for* us, but it is certainly relevant *to* us. Therefore, to truly grasp the essence of scripture, we must understand the context in which it was written.

As we read His words, we must remember that Jesus spoke these words in the 1st century AD. Semantics change over generations, and we must keep that in mind. For example, the word "gay" meant happy a few decades ago, while today, it refers to a person with a particular sexual orientation. So, to interpret scripture more accurately, we need to understand the words used in the context of time and culture. We must also understand and apply its true meaning in context, not treat imagery or words with 21st-century semantics. If we do this, we will be entirely off the mark in our understanding, interpretation and application.

IN BUT NOT OF THIS WORLD

The turning point in history was when Jesus was ushering in His kingdom. Jesus' death and resurrection ushered in a new humanity called the New Creation with a new Kingdom mandate. This new Kingdom does not force itself on us through a physical invasion; we must forcefully pursue it in our hearts. It sounds like Jesus is using a play on words, and what He said turned things upside down or commanded the opposite of what the people hoped a Messiah King would do. On the contrary, we need to seek the Kingdom and not seek a kingdom that would invade others. We must lay hold of it. Jesus gave us clues about how we seek His Kingdom, what it is like, and why it is crucial.

In this Kingdom, the King does not lord it over the others. This Kingdom does not force itself upon others. It is quite the opposite. We must vigorously and passionately pursue the Kingdom of God to benefit from it. We needs to grab hold of it forcefully or with intentionality.

Can you see Jesus provoking their minds to think in an upside-down way? They were experiencing great force and violence at the hands of their invaders. Moreover, Jesus, tongue and cheek, says if you want the Kingdom of God, you will need to come and embrace it forcefully (Matt 11:12), but not in the way you think! Jesus brought in an age of true enlightenment because He opened the scriptures up to His disciples and showed them how they needed to understand and apply them.

PARABLES ABOUT THE KINGDOM

While people in those days were familiar with what a kingdom looked like from an earthly perspective, they had no idea that the Kingdom Jesus was ushering in was different. Jesus used parable after parable, metaphor after metaphor, to describe the Kingdom of God, each giving a clue as to what it is like. Here are a few:

It is like a hidden treasure in a field (Matt 13:44)

It is like a pearl of great price (Matt 13:45-46)

It is like a house full of old and new treasures (Matt 13:52)

It is like yeast (Matt 13:33)

It is like a mustard seed (Matt 13:31-32)

It is like a seed scattered and grows by itself (Mark 4:26-29)

It is like a net that catches all sorts of fish (Matt 13:47-50)

One of the metaphors Jesus uses is of a farmer sowing in a field. The growth of the Kingdom of God will also be like the being sown in a field. Jesus says we are like seeds sown into the world.Christians often think you must get as far away from the world as possible to be distinct or holy. Jesus said exactly the opposite. He prayed that we would not be taken out of the world, but rather, just as the Father sent Jesus into the world, He said, I am sending you. So, we are sown into the world for Kingdom purposes by Jesus Himself.

I realise that whatever I do, wherever I am, I should not think of it as, "Oh, I have chosen to live in this city or chosen this career". Instead, think of it as Jesus has sown me here. Sometimes, your job may not let you attend the Sunday or mid-week meeting. Remember, Jesus has sown you into the world for a purpose. He has sown us everywhere, sometimes in cities or nations other than our birthplace.

ALREADY AND NOT YET - WHERE IS THE KINGDOM NOW?

People ask, "Will things get better or worse before Jesus' return?" The answer is both. The enemy, the devil, is at work as well. Jesus is saying that the growth of the Kingdom of God and darkness will happen together. Some people think that if only the Kingdom of God grew, there would be no evil in the world. Is that true? It is reminiscent of the picture of the wheat and the tares (weeds) growing side by side (Matt 13:24-43). Indeed, the Kingdom will grow, but along with it, the tares might also destroy some of the good of the Kingdom. There will be a simultaneous see-saw until the gospel reaches the ends of the earth.

Both the Church and the problems in the world grow side by side. Sometimes, the Church gets affected by what the enemy is doing because the tares look like wheat, and we get confused. Racism, materialism, corruption, and humanistic teaching can enter the Church. That is why we must keep pursuing Kingdom righteousness in all we do to bring His will and culture here. Know that in the end the Kingdom of God will prevail and Satan's kingdom will be defeated.

The picture you get through Jesus' teaching is that the Kingdom of God had come with Jesus' coming to earth, and still, there is an element yet to come. So, it has come and will come, meaning that while the Kingdom has come, it has not come in its entirety. There is still a fallen world we contend with. One day, when Jesus returns, His Kingdom's reign shall be over everything forever. Satan will once and for all be defeated.

Jesus says the *"Kingdom of God is at hand"* meaning it is almost here. In Luke 17:21, He says the Kingdom of God is among you. He was referring to Himself, but they did not understand it yet.

So, to answer the question of 'Where is the Kingdom now?', the answer would be that -

The Kingdom is a **present reality**: 'The kingdom of God has come upon you", Matt. 12:28); 21:31; Mark 10:15)

It is a **future blessing** (1 Cor. 15:50; Matt. 8:11; Luke 12:32),

The Kingdom is a **spiritual and saving blessing of new life** (Rom. 14:17; John 3:3) and

The Kingdom is an **expanded future rule** of society (Rev. 11:15).

THE LAW, THE KINGDOM AND THE CROSS

The new Era of the Kingdom has a new blueprint to follow. Jesus was inviting people into His kingdom, where one did not live by the law etched on stone but brandished on one's heart by the Spirit. Our intimacy with God is critical in the Kingdom. We must hear His voice and submit everything we do to the Holy Spirit and the principles in scripture. That is the beauty of being led by the Spirit; there is no 'one size fits all'.

Is Jesus doing away with the law? Far from it! Jesus said, "*I have not come to abolish the law but to fulfil it*". He showed us how to understand the law and live by it. Jesus is the Word from the beginning. Would He cancel Himself? The Law is the Word of God that has now made His dwelling amongst humanity, and He was going to show them how to live according to His Word!

Also, in our broken humanity, we could never keep the whole law. Jesus came to become the fulfilment of the law by becoming the perfect, spotless Lamb that was slain. Jesus' death on the Cross satisfied the justice of God, thus fulfilling it. We have been playing a game all wrong because we have misinterpreted the rules. Then, finally, the person who created the game comes along. He does not discard the game but shows how it should be played by explaining how the rules must be understood and applied. The Kingdom is not about rules or rituals, but it is about how we relate to the King, His subjects, and those outside of this Kingdom.

KINGDOM WAY

This Kingdom has its own King, Jesus. Its subjects are us, and it has a culture and currency of forgiveness and love. When we accept Jesus's Lordship, we become citizens of His kingdom.

In both the accounts of the Sermon on the Mount (Matthew and Luke), we see Jesus contrasting two ways: one that leads to life and the other that leads to death, two trees where one produces good fruit and the other bad, the way one prays behind closed doors and the other in the public square, the way one gives to be noticed and the other who gives everything they have. We could make the mistake of thinking that Jesus was contrasting the believer, Jew and non-believer. Jesus contrasted the way of the Pharisees, who did not interpret the Law correctly or practise it the way it ought to have. That is why Jesus says He has not come to abolish the Law but to fulfil it as it should have been done the Kingdom way. The former way was toxic religion that did not care for its fellowmen, and the latter was about loving God and people, thus fulfilling the whole Law. That is why Jesus starts His teaching with. *"Repent for the kingdom of God is at hand"*, meaning that you will need to turn away from the familiar and, 'you will have to change the way you think' for your behaviour to change as well. So, it is not just upside down but inside out as well!

CHAPTER V

THE CHURCH AND THE KINGDOM

JESUS THE HEAD OF THE CHURCH

Where does the church fit in the Kingdom? The Kingdom of God is everything Jesus is. Jesus is the King of His Kingdom and the Head of the church. Our understanding affects how we see the growth of the Kingdom. There will be ebbs and flows in a local area or a zoomed-in view, but the picture has only gotten bigger if you zoom out. The Notre Dame cornerstone was laid in 1163 and completed in 1345. It took a long time. They were not in a hurry. Many generations were involved in building it. Only one generation saw their work completed. From this, I learned that while I might not see the whole picture or be in the middle of its progress, I need to continue to do the work of the Kingdom with faith, just like the heroes mentioned in chapter eleven of Hebrews. Does the church, the apostolic vehicle for the Kingdom, have a long-term view of things? Do we have plans for how we want to infuse education, science, medicine, commerce, politics, defence, etc., with Kingdom values? Or are we stuck in our little silos trying to grow our flock, fame and name?

Great pioneers like William Carrey and Frazer had to wait seven years before they saw the fruits of their labour. They suffered great hardships and lost properties and the lives of loved ones but persevered. The fruit of their labour can now be seen in the millions of souls saved over generations. The Kingdom of God, therefore, considers a multi-generational view of things. We need to keep our eyes on and work with all age groups, and in doing so, we will ensure that our work out-lives us.

OUR STORY

We may think twenty years is a long time, but life has changed so much in the twenty years since we moved to the city where we live! The city has transformed from a sleepy town for retired army personnel to a booming IT Hub.

It took us seven years to see a breakthrough in this new city. We would be happy to see 25 people turn up on a Sunday for the first seven years of planting this church! Then, we slowly began to see a breakthrough. Twenty years on, we have seen more than 1000 people participate in Word of Grace Church and move on. We have trained many in leadership, worship leading, and preaching, knowing that they will not be with us long-term. We broadened our vision to the ends of the earth and gave them our best while they sojourned with us. We have seen scores put their faith in Jesus. It took time and patience.

High mobility amongst the IT folk has resulted in hundreds of people walking through our church doors, being discipled, and then deployed across the globe. So, zooming out and taking a long-term view allows us to embrace the churn because we are advancing God's kingdom.

In the end, the righteous will shine like the sun in the Kingdom of their Father. So, we need to shine where Jesus has placed us. However, looking back, I think we could have engaged better with our city. It is not too late; we are trying to turn this ship around by having a vision for our city and country in all walks of life.

WHERE DOES THE CHURCH FIT IN?

What is the role of the Church concerning the Kingdom of God? The Kingdom of God is the top priority. Jesus told us to seek the Kingdom *first* (Matt 6:33) and to pray, "Your kingdom come, your will be done."

The Church is the agent that ushers in the Kingdom of God. The Church is the model or prototype for people to experience the Kingdom of God here on earth. The Church is the Apostolic representation of the Kingdom of God here on earth. We are here to declare God's goodness (1 Pet 2:9). We are to be His witnesses (Acts 1:6-8). We usher in the Kingdom through preaching the gospel and expressing God's Kingdom through culture, lifestyle, commerce, justice, creativity, family, marriage, science, etc.

The Church is not comprised of people who have only experienced salvation. We are the New Creations, a holy nation, and citizens with a royal vocation.(1Pet 2:9)

> *"The Church is to be a new society where the world can see what family dynamics, business practices, race relations, and all of life can be under the kingship of Jesus Christ. God wants to heal all the effects of sin: psychological, social, and physical. -*
> *Robert Sagers"*

Some ask, can I do without a church because I am part of the Kingdom? Is it like saying, I know how to shoot a gun, so can I go to the border and defend my country? No. You have no authority to do so. You need to join the army to put that skill to proper use. You may know many things, but God has chosen us to function within the Church in His wisdom. The Church is the legitimate means to exercise your gifts and influence and favour God. Also, we cannot love Jesus and disconnect from His body. It is a contradiction.

KINGDOM APOSTOLIC MANDATE

The Kingdom of God is apostolic. An apostle is a person who shapes and facilitates cultural transformation. An apostolic people live out that knowledge and mandate to affect and influence change. They model the life and change they want to bring about. Apostolic people will be the salt in the community, bringing flavour and light that dispels darkness.

Jesus spoke about the Kingdom of God 127 times and the church only twice. The Kingdom is larger than the church; however, without the church, there would be no Kingdom advancement. Over the centuries, the church has forgotten the reason for her existence; she has forgotten her apostolic mandate. Instead of going into stormy waters and rescuing people from capsized ships and from drowning, it has become a lighthouse club for the exclusive, where we care for each other, eat together, and plan events for the young, the teens, the mothers, the old, men's breakfast club etc.

I think about a right-wing radical group in my nation, and I marvel at their foresight and meticulous planning. They are truly visionary and apostolic for their cause. They knew that to control the country and ideology, you needed to infiltrate and influence every sphere of the country, from education to engineering to commerce to industry to medicine, science, legislature, politics, and the judiciary. And by Jove, they have done it. It took perseverance, patient transformation work, and equipping its followers for several decades. When creating apostolic impact, do we have decadal plans for the church in this manner?

When we bring the Kingdom of God to earth, we can experience a measure of heaven here and now on earth. God's desire has always been for His people to shine and be His glory and image-bearers. Today that is you and I.

TREASURE IN JARS OF CLAY

This apostolic mandate existed even in the Old Testament and is expressed in Isaiah 61: to preach the good news, bind up the brokenhearted, set the captive free, and proclaim the year of the Lord's favour.

The Spirit of the Sovereign Lord is on me,
Because the Lord has anointed me
*To **proclaim good news** to the poor.*
*He has sent me to **bind up the broken-hearted,***
*to **proclaim freedom** for the captives*
And release from darkness for the prisoners,[a]
[2] *to **proclaim the year of the Lord's favour***
and the day of vengeance of our God,
*To **comfort** all who mourn,*
[3] *and **provide** for those who grieve in Zion—*
*to **bestow on them a crown** of beauty*
instead of ashes,
the oil of joy
instead of mourning,
and a garment of praise
Instead of a spirit of despair.
They will be called oaks of righteousness,
a planting of the Lord
For the display of his splendour.
[4] *They will **rebuild the ancient ruins***
And restore the places long devastated;
*They will **renew the ruined cities.***
That have been devastated for generations.

The previous chapter, Isaiah 60, tells us to *"arise and shine"* Verse 18 says God's glory would come upon us (this happens when we receive salvation) and that we will be a light to the Gentiles. *The nations will come to your light, the kings to the brightness of your dawn.* Verse four tells us the once-broken ones are coming together to rebuild ancient ruins and be world changers. We are those broken ones that will help rebuild other's lives. It is not about your blessing but about being a blessing. It is not just about your brokenness being made whole but about being the healing to the nations. It is not about looking at the darkness and feeling discouraged; it is about rising up, being that city set on a hill, and being the nation's hope.

GENERATIONAL IMPACT AND LEGACY

Scripture tells us that one generation will commend our deeds to the next.

One generation commends your works to another;
They tell of your mighty acts.
⁵ They speak of the glorious splendour of your majesty—
And I will meditate on your wonderful works.
⁶ They tell of the power of your awesome works
   (Ps 145:4-6)

From this, I understand that we are supposed to be a multi-generational movement that embraces both the young and the old. We need to have a generational mindset of leaving a legacy.

We see a tendency to do away with anyone over forty! The mindset that embraces ageism is not Biblical. The young generation is exceptionally gifted but lacks the wisdom that comes with lived experience. The older generation needs younger people to keep pace with changing technology. If both work together, we can be a formidable force. God is familial and, therefore, includes all generations in His plans. We must honour the past and learn from their wisdom which comes from life experience, being grounded in the Word and knowledge of the world's ways.

Our forefathers fought battles for the church's liberation from religious shackles, which are lost on subsequent generations that take their liberty for granted. They also invested in cultural transformation by building schools and hospitals and serving the less fortunate. Each generation has challenges and battles to contend with for The Faith.

Another Kingdom apostolic mandate is Matthew 28. Verses 18-20 command us to make disciples of all nations and teach them to obey Jesus' commands. It means we are responsible for being discipled and discipling new believers. When revival comes, all of us should get used to being activated. There are no observers and consumers in the Kingdom of God.

REDEMPTION FOR COLLABORATION

The purpose of the Kingdom of God is to restore humanity's image-bearing nature because the command to fill the earth is given to both men and women. There is no male or female emphasis, but men and women together demonstrate the rule of Christ in the right relationship with God and each other. It means that as new creations, we bring a new world order; we hold up a mirror to the world by how we live and model this new Kingdom life. We reshape and bring a new vision (just like the mandate given to Adam to name all creatures and govern over them) to world order.

Therefore, each one needs to function according to the gifts God has given us for the Church and the world. I need to allow the Kingdom of God to alter every area of my life: my choices, my character, my marriage, my family life, my attitude to work, how I engage with society, the neighbourhood, how I handle money, in short, everything. When the Kingdom infuses our lives, we start changing our culture because it will work like yeast in the dough and influence everything.

[i] 1Pet 2:9

PART 2 - THE BEATITUDES

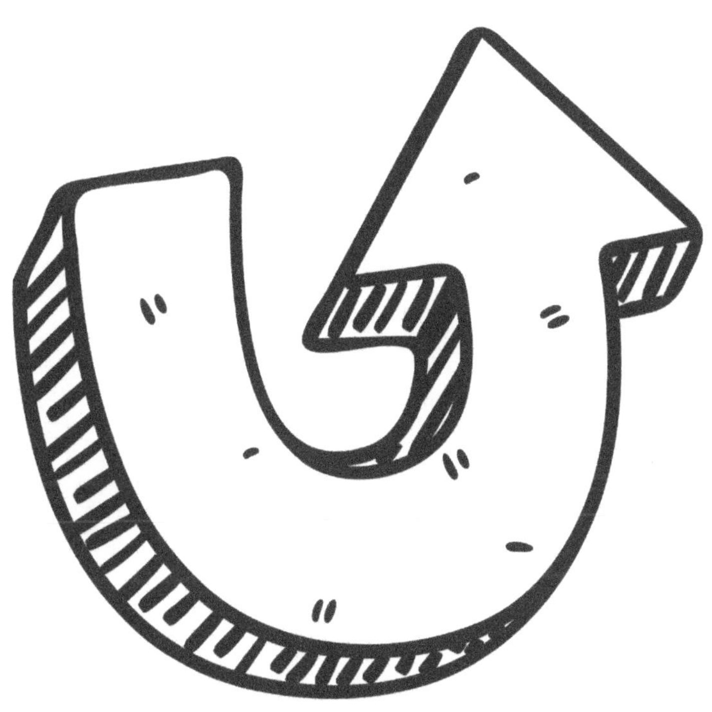

THE BEATITUDES

Jesus said:

3 "Blessed are the poor in spirit,
for theirs is the kingdom of heaven.
4 Blessed are those who mourn,
for they will be comforted.
5 Blessed are the meek,
for they will inherit the earth.
6 Blessed are those who hunger and thirst for righteousness,
for they will be filled.
7 Blessed are the merciful,
for they will be shown mercy.
8 Blessed are the pure in heart,
for they will see God.
9 Blessed are the peacemakers,
for they will be called children of God.
10 Blessed are those who are persecuted because of righteousness,
for theirs is the kingdom of heaven.

11 "Blessed are you when people insult you, persecute you and falsely
say all kinds of evil against you because of me.

Matthew 5:3-11 (NIV)

CHAPTER VI

THE BEATITUDES

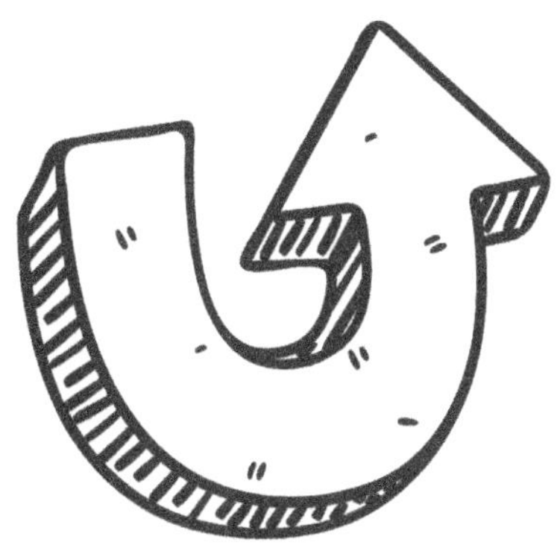

WHO IS MATTHEW?

Did you know that the label *The Sermon on the Mount* was never used in the early manuscripts? Saint Augustine of Hippo (AD 354–430) coined the title, and has been used ever since.

Now that we have explored a few characteristics of the Kingdom of God, we know how Jesus reframes the Law in the Beatitudes and the entire Sermon on the Mount. For this, I am reflecting on and studying the text as written in Matthew's accounts in chapters five to seven. Let us first take a closer look at who wrote this text. Matthew, also called Levi, is the author of this book. He was a tax collector by profession, which meant he was neither here nor there when it came to identifying and belonging to a community. The Romans employed him, and the Jews despised him, considering him a traitor who worked for the enemy. However, his profession made him very thorough and meticulous with details, documentation and recording information. Perhaps that is why he is so meticulous with the genealogy of Jesus.

As we saw earlier, Matthew mainly writes for a Jewish audience. He knew their hearts longed for the Messiah, who they hoped would come as King to overthrow their oppressors. Matthew periodically references the Old Testament to show the link between the Messiah they longed for and Jesus, God incarnate.

THE KINGDOM OF HEAVEN

In the gospel of Matthew, the 'Kingdom of Heaven', as he calls it, is a central running motif or theme. Matthew is telling his Jewish readers that Jesus was King and came to establish His kingdom, but not how they expected it.

Matthew calls it the Kingdom *"of Heaven"* and not *"of God"* because he was writing to a Jewish audience. He was being careful of the cultural and religious sensitivities to avoid offending His readers in any way that could distract them from the main message He was intent on communicating. The Jews were very careful about using the name of God; therefore, Matthew uses the term Kingdom of Heaven unlike Luke who wrote for a Gentile audience.

There is a lesson here for me to take note of. Am I aware of my cultural context and sensitive in how I share the message of Jesus? I need to be culturally relevant without being Biblically irreverent. Gospel contextualisation is vital to reaching our societies without compromise or deviation from the truth. Matthew did not dilute the message but took the trouble to find a way to say things in a palatable way. So, while the gospel does not change, I become all things to all men (1 Cor. 9:19-23).

God always wanted a unique people to be set apart for him. Israel was His chosen people. They were supposed to be a light to the Gentiles.

"I will also make you a light for the Gentiles, that my salvation may reach to the ends of the earth."
(Is 49:6)
And nations shall come to your light,
Kings to the brightness of your rising.
(Is 60:3)

Matthew 5 to 7 explains the Kingdom culture, making many references to the Old Testament, saying, "You know this in your scriptures, but this is the real heart of the matter:" The Sermon on the Mount is a treatise replete with phrases like "you have heard it said, but I say to you…" or "You believed and lived like this, but know I am telling you how it really should be done." Jesus is describing authentic Christianity.

5:21 – You have heard that it was said, 'Do not commit murder,' – but I say even if you are angry, it is murder.

5:27- You have heard it said, 'Do not commit adultery' – but I say even if you look with lust, it is adultery of the heart.

5:33 – You have heard that you should not swear or take oaths naming things in heaven, but I say keep your word. Let your yes be yes.

5:38 You have heard it is okay to take revenge; an eye for an eye – but I say turn the other cheek and give more than asked.

5:43 You have heard it said, love your neighbour, hate your enemy- I say love your enemy and do good to them.

["]"The Sermon on the Mount is nothing but a great and grand and perfect elaboration of what our Lord called His `new commandment'. His new commandment was that we love one another even as He has loved us. If we are Christ's, and our Lord has meant that word for us, that we should love one another even as He loved us, here we are shown how to do it."
Martin Llyod Jones["]

Jesus shows them how to understand and practice the law from God's vantage point. In saying "but I say to you.", Jesus is drawing their attention to Himself. He ends the sermon in Matthew chapter seven, saying, "Everyone *who hears these words of mine and puts them into practice is like a wise man who built his house on the rock.*" Our lives are to be built on obedience to His Word. It is all about relationships and not rules.Obedience is better than all the religious sacrifices you can make.

As I think about this, I am reminded of what John said of Jesus: the Word that became flesh and dwelt among us. The law or the Word becomes 'incarnational' (flesh) in the Beatitudes when it is lived through the disciples' lives. I also think of John 15, where Jesus says, "*If you love me, you will obey my commands*". He is not throwing away the importance of obedience for some wishy-washy love! Obedience to the Torah and obedience to Jesus are still requirements today. Obedience is not old-fashioned thinking. It is at the heart of the Kingdom.

Jesus was addressing the Jews, telling them in not so many words that their history does not entitle them to salvation. Their obedience to the heart of Scripture is how to be the light God wanted them to be.

A COUNTERCULTURE

As we have seen, Jesus came to usher in an upside-down kingdom, but not in the way the Jews were expecting. In the same way, we, as Christians, should be the salt and light of this world. It is the best evangelistic tool we have. How we live glorifies the Father and is the best witness of Christ in us.

We do not belong to this world. We are *in* it, but not *of* it. We are strangers and aliens. We are soldiers who do not engage in civilian affairs. We are a peculiar nation, a people belonging to God, called out of darkness into His marvellous light. Jesus talks about His Kingdom advancing against another and that it will not be able to hold back the Kingdom of God's advance (Matt.11:12). There was a clash of kingdoms in the garden of Eden. It continues till finally; we see in Revelation that Jesus rides in as the conquering King and throws Satan and all his minions into a fiery abyss forever!

Jesus is the magnificent King we belong to, and we are supposed to create a counterculture reflecting His kingdom and reign. However, too often, the church has been too tame and too tasteless, compromising with the cultures around us so that we look no different from them. In the same way, the Jews forgot their "otherness" and consorted with the nations around them and took on the culture, practices and even worship of other Gods. They were anything but a "Holy nation". They had forgotten their uniqueness.

If we are to understand the Sermon on the Mount, we should be convinced of why Jesus talked about these issues. The Sermon on the Mount is about returning to their roots by turning away from the adulteration of the law and living authentic, righteous lives.

In Matthew 6:8, Jesus instructs His listeners, "Do not be like them," referring to the Gentiles. The whole Sermon on the Mount can also be compared with non-believers. The pagans live like this, or you have heard it said this way, but I say live like this. The pagans pray like this, but you should pray like this; the pagans run after riches, but you must seek the Kingdom.

At times, the contrast is not with Gentiles or pagans, but with the 'righteous religious' and with Jewish traditions that the Pharisees and the scribes imposed. That is why the religious rulers were infuriated with Jesus as He exposed their empty hearts.

> *"The Sermon on the Mount may justly be called the key of the whole Bible, for here Christ openeth the sum of the Old and New Testaments.*
> *W. Perkins"*

Moses gave them the law on a mountain, and Jesus gave them a life-imparting counterculture on a mountaintop. Jesus' law was not another set of laws like the Ten Commandments. Instead, it describes a culture or the character of someone who lived to please God. The Pharisees and scribes had twisted the understanding and application of the law, and now Jesus was about to set it right.

WHO IS THE SERMON ON THE MOUNT FOR?

This time on the Mount was a discipling moment for Jesus and those who followed Him. He taught them that if you want to be a part of my Kingdom, then this is how you must live.

The Sermon on the Mount deals with Christian character, influence, holiness, ambition, relationships, commitment, prayer, giving and most importantly, God as Father. Jesus rips out the cold heart of the religion drowned in rituals and replaces it with a warm beating heart that connects to God and humanity through relationships. Jesus, in His many travels, discourses and conversations with His disciples, continues to refer to different aspects of this sermon. It formed the template for a lot of His teaching that followed.

This sermon is not to be used as a code of social ethics. By this, I mean that not all of society can apply it. The Sermon was not for general consumption. While you could reduce it to a code for good living, that is not its intent, and the teaching could never be fully lived without first embracing the King of this Kingdom's culture. This was Jesus' teaching to His disciples—you need to be a part of the Kingdom to truly understand and practice this teaching.

So, we can see three sections of people being addressed. Its opening section, the "Beatitudes", is addressed to His disciples. Secondly, a more significant part of the sermon was an exposition of the Law and a rejection of the interpretation and false teachings by the teachers of the law. Thirdly, it was meant for anyone willing to be poor in spirit. The gospel was not just meant for the Jews but for all people.

PIE IN THE SKY?

Can one truly live by the Sermon on the Mount, or is it an ideal beyond our grasp? We can live it only when we are truly born-again. Flesh can only give birth to flesh, which is ridden with sin and evil. Spirit gives birth to Spirit, which leads to righteousness, peace or wholeness, and joy. The Sermon on the Mount is not a whip on our backs. We can only love like this with the Holy Spirit's help. It is something you do for God but with God living inside you.[i]

> **"Jesus did not dumb down the standard to make it easy or palatable. He was raising the bar."**

Some may argue this is too challenging a set of teachings but who said anything about it being easy? Jesus already talked about how hard it is for a rich man to enter the Kingdom of God; it is easier for a camel to pass through the eye of a needle. *"Broad is the way that leads to destruction but narrow is the path that leads to life."* He also said you must take up your cross daily and deny yourself if you want to be His disciple. Jesus did not dumb down the standard to make it easy or palatable. He was raising the bar! Is it any wonder, then, that Jesus opens the sermon with, *"Blessed are the poor in spirit, for theirs is the kingdom of heaven"?*

IS THIS SERMON RELEVANT FOR TODAY?

The obvious answer is yes, simply because *"[16] all Scripture is God-breathed and is useful for teaching, rebuking, correcting, and training in righteousness, [17] so that the servant of God may be thoroughly equipped for every good work."* (2 Tim 3:16-17).

Personally, I feel that the Sermon on the Mount applies more today than ever. We live in a time where truth has increasingly become relative, and the world is getting more and more polarized along the lines of alternate truths, leading to so much hate, prejudice, wars, and the spread of lies.

AN INVITATION

In the Sermon on the Mount, Jesus is throwing an open invitation to those who want to follow Him. The Kingdom and partnering in its reign are open to those who accept Jesus as King and desire to put the law of God into practice. Now that we have reflected upon what Jesus meant by the Kingdom of God and how the Sermon on the Mount fits in, it is time to turn our attention to the Beatitudes

[i] Preaching the Kingdom – David Guzik.

CHAPTER VII

THE POOR IN SPIRIT

"Blessed are the poor in spirit, for theirs is the kingdom of heaven."
- Matthew 5:3

We have taken care of the groundwork and are ready to dive into the Beatitudes. While we meditate on just a few verses at a time, we need to remember the sermon in its entirety. We can get lost in detail and forget what the purpose of this sermon is.

As Martin Llyod Jones says of this sermon -
"It is like a symphony. The whole is greater than the collection of its parts. If you just heard the second violin, you would say that sounds so tuneless. If you just heard the trumpets you would say, why are they making those loud bursts of notes just here and there while there are so many bars of music where they play nothing at all? Ah, but when you put it all together it is the most beautiful combination of melody and harmonies creating an amazing symphony."

THE BEATITUDES

Now when Jesus saw the crowds, He went up on a mountainside and sat down. His disciples came to him, and he began to teach them. He said: "Blessed are the poor in spirit, for theirs is the kingdom of heaven.'Matthew 5:1-3

Jesus was preaching in Galilee, the Decapolis, and the surrounding regions. He had just been healing the sick and casting out demons. He went to the mountaintop to be with His disciples and away from the crowds. This teaching was for those who wanted to follow Him. He sat down to teach, as was common in those days for the Rabbi, while the rest stood and listened.

The word 'Beatitude' does not appear in the scriptures but is used as a header for this text portion. The word Beatitude comes from the Latin word beātitūdō, which means "blessed, happy or fortunate" and was first used in the 15th century. The word describes how every Christian should live. We each ought to display all eight of the 'Beatitude' characteristics in our lives, i.e., poor in spirit, mourning over our sin, meekness, hunger for righteousness, mercy, purity in heart, being peacemakers, and being persecuted for righteousness. All eight are intertwined in many ways.

I am not surprised that "being poor in spirit" is the first beatitude, for I think all else hinges on becoming poor in spirit. Herein lies the key to living out the rest of the Beatitudes. Only when we come into the Kingdom of God can we access all we have in Christ. Christ in us gives us that power and grace to live out the rest of the Beatitudes. Moreover, the only way into the Kingdom of Heaven is to have a broken, contrite spirit (Is 51:17).

BLESSED

Everybody is in pursuit of happiness. Is that wrong? No. Here is what Jesus is saying: Do you want to be happy? Then, this is how you will find true happiness. Happiness is a by-product of the Kingdom's lifestyle. You can find happiness by being poor in spirit, mourning, being meek and hungering after righteousness.

Some think they will find it in the American dream of getting that important job, big house, fancy car, and millions in the bank. They feel they will be happy accumulating wealth, nice things, and a dream lifestyle. What a deception!

As Christ-followers, we have the secrets of the Kingdom. We ought to be the happiest people on earth because Jesus has shown us how. However, we have let the world's treasures and paradigms tug at our hearts and shape our values. The pursuit of genuine happiness should drive us into the presence of Jesus. He said our joy will be complete if we abide in Him, but do we really believe that?

Makarios, the Greek word used here, means happy and content. The first thing that strikes me is that Jesus wants us to be happy. He is not a killjoy! But is our definition and Jesus' definition of happiness the same thing? What is true happiness? Can happiness be the end goal of all things? Or could there be more to it? Happiness is a part of it, but not the whole thing. 'Blessed' also implies having favour with God, as well as a state of well-being.

> *"He who would be happy must keep to Christ's road. Blessedness is not to be found in evil, but lies in the paths of righteousness. The Beatitudes are the marks of a disciple of Christ. Charles Spurgeon."*

Interesting to also note is that in Hebrew, there is no verb like "is" or "are' after the word blessed. Therefore, some commentators say the right way to read it is not as a conditional statement but as a present reality.

So, we should read it like this: "Oh, the blessedness of the poor in spirit."

Blessedness is also a characteristic of God (1 Tim 1:11), which we can only share through our union with Christ. When we live in this manner of dependence on God, we live from the will of God. We position ourselves to receive God's favour, where we can access untold heavenly riches. All this is ours because we are in Christ.

In the Beatitudes, Jesus said you will be truly happy and content when you live with the eight core values mentioned. You will enjoy spiritual well-being and God's favour. Contentment has nothing to do with what you do or do not own. Jesus said in Luke 12:15, 'Life does not consist in an abundance of possessions.'

WHAT IS "POOR IN SPIRIT"?

The Greek word for poor is ptochos, i.e., to crouch or to cower like a beggar. Jesus, however, is not talking about material poverty but spiritual poverty. Only the 'poor in Spirit' can obtain the Kingdom of God.

Poor in spirit means I recognise that I am spiritually destitute and I need a Saviour. It means that on my own, I am morally bankrupt, and there is nothing good in me without Christ. Becoming 'poor in spirit' is not an excuse or license for self-loathing or hate, nor is it an appeal to deny our worth as human beings, as some streams of Christianity might indulge in.

It is a call to recognise my sin and desperate need for salvation. The Beatitudes act as a mirror to show me how full I am of myself and what I need is to have more of Christ in me. Therefore, I aim to have all of Christ in all of me.

""To be poor in spirit is to have humble thoughts of ourselves, of what we are, and have, and do. ... [It is] to shun all confidence in our righteousness and strength, that we may depend only on the merit of Christ and the

spirit and grace of Christ. ...The kingdom of grace is composed of such; the kingdom of glory is prepared for them."

Matthew Henry"

WHY DO I NEED TO BE 'POOR IN SPIRIT?

Unless I recognise my spiritual poverty, I will not acknowledge that I need a Saviour. Apart from Jesus, I cannot put any of the Beatitudes into practice or the rest of the Sermon on the Mount into practice.

Pride will lead me to anger, independence, folly, unforgiveness, unrighteous living, and seeking satisfaction elsewhere, which lead to all kinds of sin. Isn't this the same independence and pride that led to Adam and Eve's downfall? Now I understand why Jesus addresses this first. Unless we come to Him poor in spirit, acknowledging our broken humanity, we will never be able to see God because God opposes the proud but gives grace to the humble (James 4:6).

Jesus explains that you cannot even rely on your goodness to enter God's kingdom.

"It is not saying I am a worm or insignificant. Rather it is saying I am nothing without you, but I can be everything I am meant to be when I am fully immersed in Him."

It begins with recognizing that I have nothing worthy to bring to God. All my efforts and good works are filthy rags in His sight (Is 64:6). When I come to God, emptying myself of pride, independence, self-achievements, and work and admitting my need for Him, I am rewarded firstly with a relationship with the King and thereby Kingdom citizenship.

Here is the salvation story in short.

At creation, God created Adam and Eve to have perfect fellowship with Him and to multiply and reign over the Earth and all its creatures. However, they get tempted to disobey God and fall short of the glory in which God made them; thus, corruption enters the world and affects everything. But God still wants a people for himself and makes a covenant that one day He will send a Saviour who will be a sacrifice for sin once and for all and redeem humanity back to Him. Christ Jesus becomes God incarnate who knew no sin to become sin so that we may become righteous before God. Jesus dies on the Cross for our redemption and to pay the penalty for our sins. We become a new creation in Christ.

The story does not end there. Now that we have been redeemed, God wants to restore us to our original design and purpose: to be true image bearers who once again fill the earth with God's glory. So, we are invited to collaborate with God in this amazing endeavour to take the gospel of the Kingdom of God to the ends of the earth. While things may not get fully restored and redeemed here, we will live with the tension of the Kingdom having come and not yet come. One day, when Jesus returns, there will be a final restoration of all things, and there will be a great celebration of the marriage feast of the Lamb, and we will all get to join in that celebration as the Bride of Christ.

This beatitude shows me how utterly helpless I am and that I need the daily indwelling and infilling of the Holy Spirit to maintain a poverty of spirit which says, 'I need you, Lord, more than anything'. It is not saying I am a worm or insignificant. Rather it is saying I am nothing without you, but I can be everything I am meant to be when fully immersed in Christ. The "poor in spirit" like Zacchaeus received the kingdom. After being poor in spirit, you can mourn, be meek, thirst after righteousness or be merciful to others.

SO, WHAT DO I DO TO BECOME "POOR IN SPIRIT"?

This cannot happen unless I humble myself. Humility will keep me dependent and trusting God to meet my every need, be it physical, mental, emotional, spiritual, or material. I need to come to Jesus, poor in spirit and not with a poverty spirit. Yes, there is a difference. The former comes in a posture of humility, saying that I need the One greater than me and acknowledging the all-sufficiency of the Saviour. The latter says I live in lack, and what I have is insufficient and, by virtue, denies the all-sufficiency of the Saviour. 'Poor in spirit' says I am incapable of saving myself; therefore, I need to put my trust in the all-sufficient saving power of Jesus.

> *"I need to come to Jesus' poor in spirit and not in a poverty spirit."*

Being dependent on someone grates against the high value of individualism and independence that the culture we live in promotes and applauds. Self-reliance, self-confidence, self-effort, self-promotion and the so-called self-made, Maria from the Sound of Music sings, 'I have confidence in me'. Self-reliance, however, is not the heart of a follower of Christ.

Paul says, "I have been crucified with Christ, and I no longer live, but Christ lives in me. The life I now live in the body, I live by faith in the Son of God, who loved me and gave Himself for me.'" Gal 2:20)

Paul considered all his achievements as dung compared to knowing Jesus. In Philippians, Paul says, "What is more, I consider everything a loss because of the surpassing worth of knowing Christ Jesus my Lord, for whose sake I have lost all things. I consider them garbage, that I may gain Christ" Phil 3:8). Paul boasted in his weakness so that God's power would be demonstrated through his life. We, being poor in spirit, should do the same.

HOW DO I REMAIN "POOR IN SPIRIT"?

Becoming "poor in spirit" is a character trait, not something I do. It is a heart posture that needs to be cultivated. My humanity will tug in the direction of self-will and self-reliance. Jesus said of Himself that He only did what He was the Father doing. I need to learn to live in tune with the Holy Spirit and only do what He wants me to do. I must live with the conviction that total abiding in Jesus is life-giving and a fruitful way to live. It simply means that I need the Saviour every moment of the day, and I can never bring about my salvation.

WHAT IS THE RESULT?

"For theirs is the kingdom of heaven."Matt 5:3
If we have understood the word Kingdom correctly, it should mean that the rulership of the Kingdom of God is ours. This ties in with Matthew 20, which says, 'The one who wants to lead must be the servant of all.' In the hierarchy of the kingdom, it is the humble and lowly who lead. The Kingdom does not just invite us in, but we also get to reign and rule, which is a restoration of our kingdom vocation lost in Eden. We are called to reign alongside Jesus as His coheirs.

KEY TURNING POINTS

I can only live in the Kingdom when Jesus is the King of my heart. I must live in awe of the finished work of the Cross.
Rejoice that the Kingdom of Heaven is mine.
I must be thankful for His grace in my life.
I will depend on the Holy Spirit, causing my Prayer life to grow.
I will not think highly of myself.
I will turn from pride-filled, self-reliant ways and serve with humility because no task is too small for me.

I will love as Christ loves.

REFLECTIONS

- How aware am I of the need to be poor in spirit?
- Do I take everything to God in prayer, or do I try to sort things out on my own first?
- Am I open to asking for help, or do I insist on struggling alone because I am too proud to ask for help or admit any weakness?

ACTION PAGE
What knowledge can I rejoice in?
What is the Holy Spirit convicting me of?
What will I change in my beliefs, thougts and actions?

CHAPTER VIII

THE MOURNERS

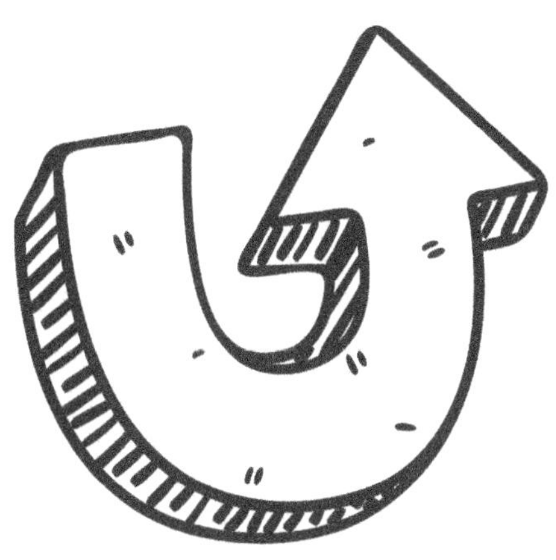

"Blessed are those who mourn, for they shall be comforted."
Matthew 5:4

"Oh, how blessed are you when you mourn!!" Does this not sound strange? What a peculiar blessing, and for an even stranger reason! One usually associates mourning with significant loss, the death of a loved one, or tremendous heartache which is nothing close to being blessed.

This beatitude reflects Kingdom culture since Jesus is teaching about the nature of the Kingdom. Jesus is showing us eight Kingdom characteristics that we need to imbibe, not one-time events we might engage in.

Repentance and renewal are ongoing processes in our lives. The more I gaze into the face of Christ, the more I will become aware of my failings and, yes, even grieve over how my sin has caused pain to God and others. A broken and contrite heart will mourn over sin and how it has grieved God's heart.

WHAT AM I SUPPOSED TO MOURN OVER?

I need to mourn over my sinful state. When I realise how poor in Spirit, how needy and how depraved I am without the love of Christ within us, I will mourn over our condition and recognise my need for a Saviour. The proud are blind to their faults, so they cannot come to God as poor in Spirit and can never truly mourn. I need to be sorrowful about my sinful habits.

Is this mourning related to salvation? This mourning could be in the context of saving faith or salvation, but it is more than that. I come to salvation poor in spirit, mourning over my sinful, hapless state. This drives me to look upward to a Saviour who can and "will make an end to all my sins"[i] because of His death on the Cross.

I also need to weep with those who weep and mourn with those who mourn (Rom 12:15). The Kingdom is about putting others first and above us. As we receive God's comfort, we ought to become that incarnational comfort to others. When I read Romans 12 where Paul gives some practical advice, you will notice that he is reiterating the Sermon on the Mount, showing how to practise kingdom life in the newly founded Ecclesia or church.

"Jesus says blessed are those who mourn because they recognize the brokenness of the world and their own hearts. It's only through this deep realization that we can be comforted by the gospel. Tim Keller"

Ecclesiastes 3:1, 4 reminds us that there is a time to mourn and a time to dance. The prophets of old mourned over the state of Jerusalem, and Jesus did the same in Matthew 23:37. I ask myself; do I mourn over the condition of my city and nation? Or do I complain and grumble? I am guilty of the latter. I will only mourn over my nation's state when I realise God's heart for the world. I will mourn along with God, whose heart weeps over His creation. I must mourn the injustices in my city, nation, and world, for there are so many viz. poverty, crime, hate, atrocities against women and children, widespread corruption and more. Do these move my heart to prayer and action? I need to repent for my apathy, engage with the city, and feel the pain of its needs. I need to move from just tongue-clicking and turn to compassionate action.

Jerusalem is a picture of both God's holy city and His people. We, the ecclesia, are the new Jerusalem! Do I mourn over the plight of the church? So many have strayed away, lost their vision, slipped into mindless tradition devoid of the Spirit, and gotten locked and lost in a quagmire of legalism. Instead of being a place of Shalom, there has been much abuse of power, money, and sex. Do I mourn that, at times, the church has become unsafe? Jesus took a whip and drove out the corrupt money changers who made His Father's house into a den of thieves. Have we robbed God of the glory due to Him and made the church about everything but His presence?

WHAT KIND OF MOURNING?

As you look at scripture, you will notice two types of mourning: godly and worldly. What is the difference? The difference is the fruit it produces.

Godly sorrow results in true repentance, a conviction that leads to seeking God's forgiveness and then turning away from wrong beliefs. This could lead to a change in behaviour. We see this godly repentance in King David's life. When the prophet confronted him with his sin, he acknowledged it and was deeply sorrowful. He sought God's forgiveness and repented before the people in the temple. In Psalm 51, he cries, "Against you, you only, have I sinned."

By contrast, worldly sorrow will display remorse, regret, and, yes, a type of mourning, but it will not lead to repentance. It might even produce a confession, but it alone does not lead to repentance. Confession is only an admission of guilt. There is no sorrow over how one's actions have hurt others or even the heart of God. One may mourn, but the mourning might be about what one has lost rather than one's sinful action.

I have met people like this. Their sin caught up with them. They expressed much remorse through tears, but there was no real conviction of sin. They were preoccupied with how they would manage the consequences of their sin rather than come to God, poor in spirit, make a U-turn, and have a fresh start.

Godly sorrow focuses on how sin could have affected others and how it has grieved the heart of God, whereas worldly sorrow focuses on oneself and what one stands to lose. King Saul and Judas are examples of worldly sorrow. Both did not turn to God and acknowledge their sin before God. Saul tried to justify his sin, saying the people had forced him to bring back some of the spoils of war. In plain words, justification is an attempt at a "cover-up". Instead of acknowledging his sin, Saul begged the prophet not to expose him before the people. He was more interested in saving face. Judas' remorse resulted in him hanging himself because his self-loathing and shame did not allow him to experience the grace of the Saviour. It is sobering to note that though Judas lived with Jesus for three years, he never understood His heart. By contrast, Peter, after his denying Christ, ran towards Jesus rather than away and was restored.

MATT 5:3b "FOR THEY SHALL BE COMFORTED."

We talk of comfort food, our comfort zone, our comfort place, etc. Comfort implies a place, a situation, or a substance that makes us feel relaxed and without stress. The comfort that the Bible talks about is much more than that. The promise of comfort is so beautiful, even though it does not say our mourning will cease. We need to ask ourselves what is the nature of the comfort promised ?

As we look at scripture, we notice that more than sixty references are made to God as the source of comfort.

In Psalm 23:4 God's presence is a comfort to us.

Isaiah 40:1-2,49:13,51:12, 61:3 God assures Israel of His comfort through difficult times of hardship, affliction, and captivity.

Comfort, comfort my people, says your God. Speak tenderly to Jerusalem and proclaim to her that her hard service has been completed, that her sin has been paid for, that she has received from the Lord's hand double for all her sins. Isaiah 40:1-2

This comfort is unlike what we are used to, i.e. a brief hug, a pat on the back, a few kind words or a bowl of chicken soup. The comfort that God brings to us is Himself. In 2 Corinthians 1:3, God is described as the Father of compassion and the God of all comfort.

The Greek word for comfort is παρακαλέω *(parakaléō)*,which comes from two words:

Para means "alongside" or "beside."

Kaleo means "to call."

Together, *parakaléō* means "to call alongside. According to Strong's Greek interlinear, *Parakaléō* ("personally make a call") refers to believers *offering up evidence* that *stands up in God's court.* The word is also used for the Holy Spirit and has the same root meaning of coming along with us and helping us in our weakness.

So, God is offering us more than some reassuring words. He offers His strong presence to be with us through every trial. The Greek word means we are summoned to plead our case before God, and our Lord Jesus advocate on our behalf (1 John 2:1). This kind of comfort brings true consolation because we have a righteous Judge.

"Mourning is the marination where our heads, hearts, and hands need to become tender and attentive to the things that break the heart of God."

• • •

JESUS, THE MOURNER AND COMFORTER!

Isaiah 61 says the Messiah will comfort all who mourn and grieve in Zion. As I reflect on Scripture, it reminds me that the Lord is close to the brokenhearted and the crushed in Spirit (Ps 34:18). Jesus wept over Jerusalem (Matt 23:27). Jesus prayed with great travailing and mourning (Hebrews 5:7-8). Jesus also promises us comfort. One of the titles of Jesus is *"the consolation/comforter of Israel"* (Luke 2:25).

THE NOW AND NOT YET.

Many of David's psalms were Laments or mournful songs. An entire book in the Bible called Lamentations has a place in Scripture and records Jeremiah's mourning! The understanding that we are in a "now and not yet" time in history may challenge some Christian thought that leans towards an over-realized eschatology. It simply means that these people believe that once a person has experienced the new birth, they will only experience a victorious life because Christ has won the victory for us. Anything less means "I have not grown in my faith" or "I do not fully believe in the finished work of the Cross." I wonder how people who believe this way contend with this verse about mourning.

It is interesting to note that in all the Beatitudes, there is a new blessing and a future promise that we will experience some measure here and now, and we will also experience full comfort when we are with Jesus in heaven. While we might not see the total consolation for our mourning right now, remember that all the Beatitudes have a "here" and a "not yet" locked into their promises. The words *"they shall be comforted"* indicate a future fulfilling. It reminds me of the verse in Revelations 21:4, which says, *"He shall wipe away every tear from their eyes and death shall be no more, neither shall there be mourning"*. It means that while I live and breathe on this earth, there will be things to mourn over that might not get resolved in my lifetime, but I also live with the hope that one day, all *"mourning and sorrow shall flee away"* (Is 51:11) when we shall see Him face to face.

KEY TURNING POINTS

- The realisation of my sinfulness must result in grieving and mourning over my sin.
- Mourn over how I have grieved the heart of God.
- Check that I am expressing Godly sorrow that leads to true repentance and turning away from sin.
- Only God can bring true comfort now and then fully when we meet him face to face.

REFLECTIONS

- Have I genuinely mourned over my sinful behaviour and asked forgiveness from God?
- Do I find that, often, I try to justify my actions or cover up rather than own up?
- Do I express regret or repentance?
- Can I also mourn over the needs and pains of my city, country and church?

[i] Songwriters: Vikki Cook / Charitie Bancroft - Before the Throne of God Above lyrics © Sovereign Grace Worship

ACTION PAGE
What knowledge can I rejoice in?
What is the Holy Spirit convicting me of?
What will I change in my beliefs, thougts and actions?

CHAPTER IX

THE MEEK

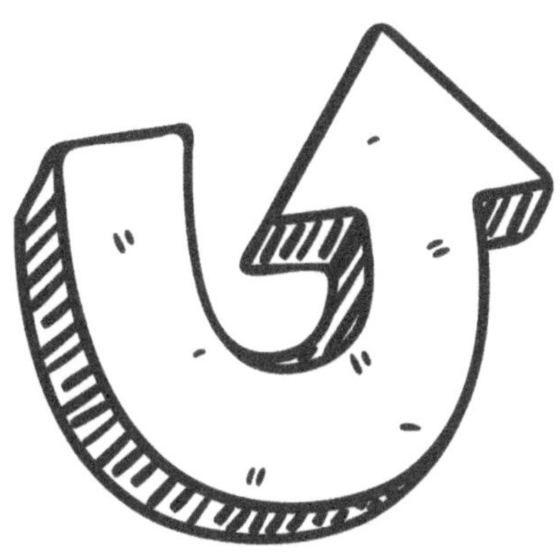

"Blessed are the meek, for they shall inherit the earth."
Matthew 5:5

As we've seen by now, the Jews were expecting a warrior Messiah to overthrow their temporal oppression but instead, Jesus came to establish a different kind of Kingdom. Jesus said that when citizens of His Kingdom practice the Beatitudes, it brings glory to the Father. Jesus' reason for coming to earth was to do the Father's will and bring Him glory. Matt 5:16 says, *"Let your light shine before men, that they may see your good works and give glory to your Father who is in heaven."* Later in the Sermon on the Mount, Jesus teaches His disciples to pray, "Our Father in heaven, hallowed be your name.". Jesus' passion was to glorify the Father, which should be ours as well. Philippians 2 tells us that Jesus lowered and humbled Himself and became obedient to death for the glory of the Father. Let us look at the next Beatitude.

Blessed are the meek, for they shall inherit the earth. Matt 5:5

This beatitude is probably a reference to Psalm 37, which the Jews would have recognised.

Ps 37:9 - "But those who hope in the Lord will inherit the land. But the meek will inherit the landand enjoy peace and prosperity."

Jesus draws on familiar Old Testament teachings to show the Jews the heart of the scriptures they had been "following." The Pharisees added so many additional rules, regulations, and laws that the yoke of human tradition obscured the original law and intent. That is why when Jesus starts His Sermon on the Mount, He shocks them with the eight beatitudes about what truly makes people blessed in His Kingdom. This is the opposite of their life experience and what they sought in Messiah's Kingdom.

Picture a terrorist with a gun and a soldier with a gun. Picture a wild, untamed stallion and a racehorse. Both men have guns. Both horses are strong and fast. Do any of them appear meek? To answer that, let us understand what 'meekness' means.

MEEKNESS

The Greek word is *Praus*. 'Meekness' implies a powerful personality that is adequately *controlled and humble*. The Greek understanding follows the idea of a stallion that is 'broken in' and in control. However, that is not what we think of at all. We picture a meek person who is passive or a 'pushover'.

Did you know a soldier must learn to become meek? A good soldier is meek – he trains to fight, kill, subdue, and protect land, but *only* at the command of his General or superior. He could do all this independently, but every army that intends to win a war needs soldiers who are meek.

How is meekness different from humility? Humility is how we look at ourselves in that we have a sober judgement of who we are and what we can and cannot do. Meekness is about how we relate to people.

WHAT IS MEEKNESS?

Meekness is not a personality trait. None of us are naturally or inherently meek. We cultivate this character trait in the counterculture Kingdom of God.

MEEKNESS IS NOT

Weakness – Being meek does not mean you are not a pushover or a doormat. It is not a lack of convictions. It is not fence-sitting and saying, "Your truth is your truth, and my truth is my truth."

Being Quiet - Meekness is not being quiet. Reticent people can be arrogant, stubborn, and unsubmitted to God. I have also seen the 'loud extrovert, natural-born leader' be very meek in surrendering their life to God. The meek can get angry and not sin. The meek can suffer wrong without getting bitter.

MEEKNESS IS:

1. **Trusting** - Psalms 37:9-11 shows the meek *"hope in the Lord"* and "wait" for Him. They do not put their confidence in their strength or strategies. They are dependent on God to lead them and bring deliverance.
2. **Waiting** - Psalms 37:5 says, *"Commit your way to the Lord; trust in him, and he will do this: He will make your righteous reward shine like the dawn, your vindication like the noonday sun."* Hope often requires "waiting". Waiting is not passive. We are meant to continue to live life, seeking God's Kingdom and seeking His ways, knowing that at the right time, He will fulfil the desires

of our hearts. Our faith is not transactional. We are not God's equal to dictate terms to Him. Many Christians have an "if-then" relationship with God, which is unscriptural. We need an *"even-if"* relationship like the three men in the fire (Daniel 3). Now, that is meekness! We must learn to wait as we surrender our will to God for Him to act on in His time.

3. **Refraining from revenge** -*"Love must be sincere. Hate what is evil; cling to what is good."* (Romans 12:9). We are often reminded not to fret or to take matters into our own hands when evil men do wicked things. It takes more courage, strength and self-control to love than to hate. Hate does not require much energy or any self-control. Jesus, further on, tells His disciples to love their enemies, pray for them, and show them kindness. He expounds on what true meekness is. Jesus displayed meekness when He told Judas to go and do what he needed to on that dreadful night of His betrayal. (John 13:27)

4. **Slow to speak** - James 1:19-21 says, *"Know this, my beloved brethren. Let every man be quick to hear, slow to speak, slow to anger, for man's anger does not work the righteousness of God. Therefore, put away all filthiness and rank growth of wickedness and receive with meekness the implanted word, which can save your souls."*

   When we lack meekness, we are quick-tongued and quick-tempered. We want to push our own opinions rather than submit and learn. Does slow to speak mean you are always soft-spoken? No. Jesus was meek, yet He drove out the money changers with a whip. Did He calmly say, "Could you please take your business elsewhere? I would be much obliged if you did?". No! He told them to get out!

5. **Quick to listen** - James 1:19: *"Know this, my beloved brethren. Let every man be quick to hear.* A meek person is quick to listen. They know their limitations and accept their faults. The person is not angered when they do not get their way or when people have different opinions from theirs.

   You can be amidst a conflict and still be meek – if you are quick to listen, slow to speak, and open to another's opinion.

6. **Teachable** - *"He guides the humble in what is right and teaches them his way." Psalms 25:9.* The meek are teachable because they have a sober judgement of themselves and are open to counsel and correction. How do you react? Do you kick back like a wild stallion, play the blame game, sulk, and pity yourself, or can we follow the example of Jesus in Philippians 2? Jesus, though He was the son of God, learned obedience through the things He suffered. Therefore, God exalted him. The way up is down. The Son of God became incarnate to show humans how to be truly human the way God intended.

7. **Broken** - The meek are broken at the Cross. When they see the depravity of their sin and mourn over it and how it has grieved the heart of God, they are led to repentance and a *brokenness* that makes us whole. We all have a brokenness that is a part of our humanity. That brokenness produces the opposite of meekness. It leads to all the sins we can think of and can cause damage to our relationships. The brokenness that comes from dying to self and letting God work in our lives produces a harvest of righteousness, peace and joy. It is like a wild stallion whose strength has been 'broken in' and now has excellent use.

8. **Wise** - *"Who is wise and understanding among you? Let him show by good conduct that his works are done in the meekness of wisdom." James 3:13*

   A wise person is a meek person. James tells us that a wise person is peaceable, gentle, and open to reason. These are qualities of a meek person as well. The teachable are wise, and because they are wise, they are teachable. When was the last time someone could give you feedback, and you accepted it? When was the last time you openly invited feedback and did not shoot the messenger?

9. **Defends the truth** -Meekness submits to and seeks truth in every situation. Meekness stands for righteousness and truth, no matter the cost (1 Pet 3:15-16). Meekness is the willingness to submit our thoughts and opinions to a higher moral standard.

The Bible is our plumbline. Where do you stand in conflict? Do you seek the truth, or are you only looking to defend yourself?

"True biblical meekness is a self-control of strength that makes us lambs in our causes and lions for the cause of Christ."
Matthew Henry

THEY "SHALL INHERIT THE EARTH".

The world tells you the meek are weak, that they are losers. They say, "You will never get ahead in life if you are meek. You need to be aggressive and assertive and promote yourself in the eyes of the boss, or you will not get noticed."

Despite that narrative, Jesus says that we, the meek, will inherit the earth. Is this a new thought? No! God's plan and design in the Garden of Eden for Adam and Eve was for them to have dominion over the earth. However, they forfeited this privilege in the Fall.

Humans would have remained in charge if Adam and Eve lived with meekness towards God, surrendering and submitting to His will. We all know what happened instead.

Jesus came to glorify the Father, to reveal Him and restore us to sonship. When we live with meekness towards God, God will once again entrust all things to us. As co-heirs with Christ, we reign and sit with Him in the heavenly places. However, the measure to which we can rule and have authority is tied to our meekness! Demons will bow to us *when* we bow to Jesus. We can command sickness to flee *when* we are under the command of the Captain of the Hosts - Jesus.

Now, is this inheritance a physical one? Does this mean you may claim any land that is yours? The Jews misunderstood the rule and reign of the Messiah. They wanted a physical conqueror when not even the Old Testament described the Messiah this way. If you read Isaiah, you will see the Messiah portrayed as meek.

Isaiah 42:2: *"He will not shout, cry, or raise his voice in the streets."*

It was there all along, but they did not want to see it. What can we learn from this? Do not try to make God in your image or conform Him to a figment of your imagination. We try to do this more than we realise when we say things like, "God will do this for me when I tell Him to do so." or "He must deal with my boss the way I want him to." or "He will sort out my husband/wife how I want Him to." or "God will never send people to hell", or "God understands because He is a loving God".

EXAMPLES OF MEEKNESS

Jesus said, *"Take my yoke upon you and learn of me; for I am meek and lowly in heart: and you shall find rest unto your souls."* Matt 11:29

Jesus demonstrated his meekness by saying, 'I only do what I see my Father doing.' We see Christ living out meekness flawlessly, emptying Himself as He carries out His Father's will. Meekness turned the tables in the temple, showed compassion to the crowds, called the Pharisees a brood of vipers, and prayed, "Not my will, but yours, be done."

"Increasing meekness is merely a reflection of our Immanuel."
Matthew Henry

Meekness characterises the Lion of the tribe of Judah and the Slain Lamb. It is meekness that carries out the Trinity's plan for our salvation. Jesus in the garden of Gethsemane epitomised meekness. He was in total surrender even though He could command a legion of angels to rescue Him. Jesus demonstrated His power by healing the soldier's ear. He was showing them what he could do but chose not to do. That is meekness.

Moses was considered the meekest man who lived (Num 12:3), yet he faced off against Pharaoh. Moses, the Pharaoh's son, was not meek. He killed an enslaved person in the name of justice.

Forty years later, Moses comes back meek and leads millions out of slavery. In his strength, he saved one. Surrendered, he saved millions.

Abraham was meek – When Lot's flock and his herd grew too large for the land they were sharing, he did not assert his authority as the elder over Lot but let his nephew choose where he would like to settle first. (Gen 13)

David allowed himself to be ill-treated by King Saul when he suffered injustice and unkind treatment. He did not take the chances he had to kill Saul but was meek and respected Saul's position as King. (1 Samuel)

Stephen was meek, and Paul, the "least of the apostles," was meek. Nevertheless, they spoke up boldly when required. They healed the sick and spread the gospel, and both were martyred.

God wants us as sons and daughters to rule the earth once again. How? By becoming meek. By becoming salt and light. Neither element draws attention to itself, but both bring change and influence their atmosphere subtly and inconspicuously.

Meekness is not easy. Without becoming poor in spirit, we cannot become meek. Without mourning over our pride and independence, we cannot come to repentance and have a desire to change and become meek. Let us ask Jesus to grant us the grace to become meek and submit to His authority.

KEY TURNING POINTS

Meekness is a Christlike quality where:

- He will increase, and I will decrease.
- His priorities will become mine.
- What breaks His heart will break mine, too.

- I will embrace my circumstances and surrender to His will, allowing His peace to guard my heart and mind.

REFLECTIONS

- Have I seen being meek as a weakness?
- Is surrender a hard thing for me to do?
- Am I broken in for God's purposes and glory, or am I a wild stallion that will not surrender?
- How do I relate with people who are not treating me well?

ACTION PAGE
What knowledge can I rejoice in?
What is the Holy Spirit convicting me of?
What will I change in my beliefs, thougts and actions?

CHAPTER X

THE HUNGRY AND THIRSTY

*"Blessed are those who hunger and thirst for righteousness, for they
will be filled."*
Matthew 5:6

We come to the fourth beatitude. We all know physical hunger. We also have longings and yearnings. The Psalmists describe the longings of the heart and soul with poetic intensity. David writes, *"My soul longs for You, O my God...in a dry and weary land.". "As the deer pants for water, my soul longs after you..."*

Appetites can be both good and bad. The Bible talks about both. What do we crave after? Esau sold his birthright for a pot of stew. Samson sold his destiny for sexual pleasure, an appetite he had no control over. Achan cost Israel a war because of his appetite for wealth.

Jesus gives us the hallmark of a person who belongs to the Kingdom of God. What distinguishes him from the rest is his appetite. He hungers and thirsts *for righteousness*. We are told that God will satisfy us. Jesus said of Himself, *"My food is to do the will of the Father"* (John 4:34). Job said, *"I have cherished your word more than my daily bread"* (Job 23:12).

So, how do we cultivate this kind of appetite? Can anyone develop this hunger and thirst? Only the spiritually awakened can hunger and thirst after righteousness. The spiritually dead have no appetite for it. We become new creations with new desires only once made alive in Christ.

We are blessed when we hunger after righteousness. You hunger and thirst after something when you are passionate about pursuing it. It is not a casual desire. Let us examine this word a little more. The word *'righteous'* or *'righteousness'*, used in different contexts, appears more than 800 times in the Bible. To hunger after something, I need to first know about it. It is like when a friend returns from having a fancy dinner at a restaurant and describes all the delicious food laid out that you begin to desire to experience it for yourself. Until then, you were pretty happy eating fast food at the street corner.

WHAT IS RIGHTEOUSNESS?

First, it is an attribute of God. Justice and righteousness are the foundations of His throne (Psalm 89:14). We are encouraged to seek His kingdom and righteousness. God is a righteous judge. He loves righteousness and hates wickedness. God rewards righteousness in people like Noah and Abraham.

> *"The Christian's hunger and thirst is not just for personal morality but for God's righteousness to reign in the world. It's a desire for God's justice, holiness, and truth to prevail. R. C Sproul"*

In Psalm 23, God leads us on *"paths of righteousness"*. Righteousness is a character trait, a way of life, and a heart attitude with how we deal with people. Therefore, it means we must be *right* with God and people. The Pharisees were very good at being right in performing all the required rituals by law but were unrighteous and unmerciful with people. That is why Jesus said our righteousness needs to increase that of the Pharisee (Matt 5:20), i.e., it must go beyond duty-bound rituals into compassionate action. Being right with people is as important as being right with God, but we cannot do the latter without the former.

BEING RIGHT WITH GOD

We cannot talk of righteousness without talking about being right with God. The whole point of Jesus coming to earth was to sort this problem out. We had lost our standing with God because of Adam's sin. Everything we do, touch, and think about is marred by our unrighteous, sinful hearts. God, the Righteous Judge, cannot allow sin to go unpunished. Only a sinless, righteous person could pay that price for all humanity, and Jesus paid the price for us. God's people did not want a relationship with Him; they exchanged it for rules, and thus, the law came through Moses. God knew the law was the schoolmaster that would lead them to grace in His son, Jesus (Gal 3:24-27). On the Cross, Jesus took the penalty for our unrighteousness, and now we have a legal standing before God as righteous.

Our human righteousness is like filthy rags in God's sight that can only lead to death (Isaiah 64:6). The Father's gift is righteousness through Jesus (Rom5:17). What does this mean? It means a right standing before God or *'positional righteousness'*, i.e. we are no longer guilty or condemned.

Jesus tells Nicodemus in John 3 that unless one is *Born Again*, one cannot see the Kingdom of God! Our justification by faith, where God's loving kindness leads us to repentance, is a crucial precursor to entering the Kingdom of God. Justification puts us in the right standing with God. We must remind ourselves that Beatitudes are not a code of social ethics anyone can follow. It is the hardest to live by and cannot be lived with the empowering grace of God.

BEING RIGHT WITH PEOPLE

Wwe can only live righteous lives once we have a positional righteous standing in God, and through the power of the Holy Spirit dwelling in us. The Pharisees were terrible at treating humans with compassion. They added more laws, making it even harder for anyone to be a good Jew. That is why Jesus tells people that loving God is the greatest command, and there is a second just like it: *"Love your neighbour as yourself"* All the law and the prophets are summed in these two! Imagine that! So, living a righteous life was not about keeping religious rituals but living right by our fellow beings. If we are willing to see it, it is all in Jesus' teaching.

When Jesus read from Isaiah 61, He showed that righteous living can be fulfilled when we live to see people free from oppressive laws and injustice; we care for the poor, needy, and the brokenhearted. Righteous living means we bring back the right order of things in society. We become that Light of the world where Isaiah 60:3 says, *'Nations will come to your light, and kings to the brightness of your dawn.'* In history, we see how Christians were involved in the abolishment of slavery, the creation of better working conditions, the discovery of life-saving drugs, and inventions of all sorts. They changed and influenced every aspect of life. As Christ's followers, we must continue influencing society as this is our mandate and must be the natural outflow of our lives. Jesus said that by the fruit, you will know a tree. We are to produce fruits of righteousness, which are also one of the fruits of the Spirit.

THE RIGHT APPETITES – SOUL FOOD

As new creations in Christ, we have new appetites.

Old habits will tempt us to desire the old stuff, but as we feast on the Word of God, it will become the bread by which we live and will mean more to us than life.

How do we maintain this appetite when there is a temptation to run after attractive food that is poison for the soul and spirit? Whatever you develop an appetite for is what you will crave. If you stop eating sugar or anything made with sugar, your body eventually adapts to the new tastes so much that you might feel squeamish when you have sugar again. It is the same with soul food. As you live by the Spirit, your desires will change, and you will no longer crave the sinful stuff.

Eating and Starving

While very pleasing to the palate, junk food has little or no nutritional value. If that is all you eat, you will suffer from malnutrition. The same is true. for the spiritual. If you feed yourself on things that do not benefit your spirit, you will grow spiritually weak and sick. You will not be able to discern between what is righteous and what is not and begin to live a life of compromise. To be salt and light is to live an uncompromised life.

Satisfaction

Everyone wants to live a life of satisfaction, but not everyone knows how. Jesus answered this in the Beatitudes. When we hunger and thirst for the right things, we are satisfied. He told the Samaritan woman that she would never thirst again if she drank the water He gave her.

Isaiah 55 also mentions the invitation to thirst after only what God can give: *"Come all who are thirsty..."*

Jesus, on the last day of the great feast, cries out in a loud voice, *"If anyone is thirsty, come to me and drink..."* (John 7:37-38)

> *""To have found God and still pursue Him is the soul's paradox of love."*
> *A. W Tozer.*"

Revelation ends with this invitation: *"Come all who are thirsty, and I will give you the water of life."* (Revelations 21:6)

When I drink the water Jesus gives, I will stop craving the fake stuff. The more I drink from Him, the more I want the Holy Spirit. The more we eat of the Bread of Life, the more we desire the Word.

Unlike addiction, which leaves you wanting more of the substance that could kill you or leave you worse off when the 'high 'wears off, when we hunger and thirst for righteousness, we begin to reign in life, know true freedom and thrive.

OBEDIENCE: THE RIGHT RESPONSE

Our hunger and thirst for righteousness will result in obedience to Jesus. As I mentioned earlier, Jesus ends His sermon on the Mount with the story of the wise and foolish builder. The one who obeys is the one who is blessed. Do you have an ongoing desire for righteousness in your life? God is infinite, and our pursuit of Him and knowing Him can never end. The more we see Him, the more we realise how much we need Him. When we meet Him face to face, our hunger and thirst will be wholly quenched because Revelations says, *"Never again will they hunger; never again will they thirst. ...; he will lead them to springs of living water..."*. Until that day, let us continue to hunger and thirst after God.

KEY TURNING POINTS

- I need to hunger for the right things.
- Righteousness is to be in the right relationship with God and people.
- I need to turn away from wrong appetites.
- True satisfaction is in Jesus alone.

REFLECTIONS

- What does righteousness toward people around me look like?
- Am I unkind to my neighbours or family?
- What are my default cravings? How can I change them?
- What is my attitude towards the poor, needy and brokenhearted?

ACTION PAGE

What knowledge can I rejoice in?

What is the Holy Spirit convicting me of?

What will I change in my beliefs, thougts and actions?

CHAPTER XI

THE MERCIFUL

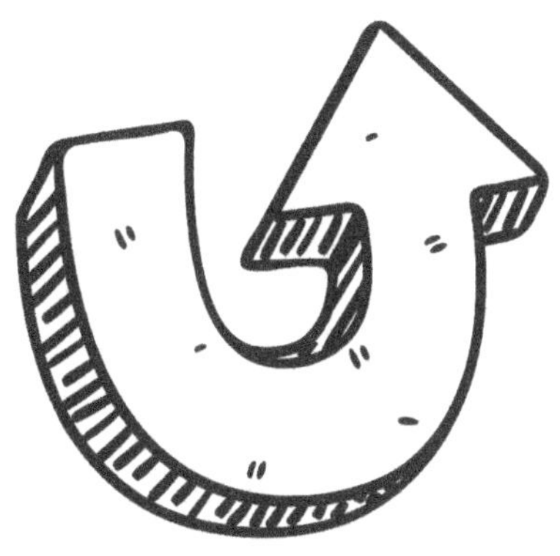

Blessed are the merciful, for they shall obtain mercy. Matt 5:7

So far, we have seen four: the poor in spirit, the mourners, the meek, and those who hunger and thirst after righteousness. The first four beatitudes are about our attitude and relationship with God. The next four are about our actions and how we relate to people. Let us look at the next beatitude. It is probably one of the most difficult to put into practice.

BLESSED ARE THE MERCIFUL

Once again, let us remember that Jesus was addressing His followers, not just any crowd. If you are in the Kingdom of God, you have already received mercy. You can only enter the Kingdom of God if you seek God's mercy. The Mercy Seat is the starting place. Mercy is not a New Testament concept. The word 'mercy' is mentioned one hundred and twenty-six times, seventy-one of which are in the Old Testament alone. It has always been around because God never changed.

Mercy is God's heartbeat. If that had not been the case, God would not have made a way for His people to receive forgiveness. We can look at all the animal sacrifices in the Old Testament and think, 'God was so harsh'. It is quite the opposite. God was providing them with a way out until the fullness of time when He sent Jesus to die and be that sacrificial lamb once and for all. So, it is mercy all the way through.

Psalms 103 reminds us that *"He does not treat us as our sins deserve."* It is interesting to note that the idea of mercy was present in the Old Testament, too. Let us never forget that. I am so thankful for His mercy over me. The gospel's central message is this: *"But because of his great love for us, God, who is rich in mercy, ⁵ made us alive with Christ even when we were dead in transgressions—it is by grace you have been saved.* We would be doomed to hell's eternal flames without the grace and mercy of God. Take a minute and thank God that He chose to have mercy on you.

The Kingdom of God is all about giving, not receiving. What we receive from God is, in turn, what we can give to others. Once we have received mercy, we can give mercy. Jesus has always been concerned with what is going on in our hearts- because we speak and act out of the overflow of the heart (Luke 6:45). That is why the first four beatitudes dealt with our hearts. From that place and only that place can we do the rest. As Tim Keller puts it, *'we are first objects of renewal and then become agents of renewal'*.

WHAT IS MERCY?

This word mercy in Greek, ἐλεήμονες *(eleēmones)*, means*"full of pity, merciful, compassionate"*andis used only twice in the New Testament. It comes from the root word *eleéō* – to show mercy as God defines it, i.e. as it accords with His truth (*covenant*), which expresses "God's covenant-loyalty-mercy" (i.e. *acting only on His* *terms*) [5] This word is used here and in Hebrews 2:16. It contrasts the Romans and the religious leaders who were merciless and saw mercy as a sign of weakness. Jesus was merciful and compassionate to the poor, the blind, the cripple, the demon-possessed, the sinners, and tax collectors. Kingdom people are mercy givers. It is a tangible attribute of a Christ follower.

IS MERCY THE SAME AS FORGIVENESS?

As we saw earlier in Ephesians 2, Mercy is an element of salvation [6]. It is behind the scenes in the salvation story. God's mercy is what makes Him save and redeem us. Mercy is, without a doubt, behind forgiveness. They belong together like two sides of the same coin.

Forgiveness is mercy in action. God's mercies are new every morning (Lam 3:23, Is 43:19). He gives us a fresh start each day. However, still, Mercy is more than just forgiveness. God, in His rich mercy, gives us a second chance, which is why we are also commanded to forgive 70x7.

MERCY AND GRACE

Why did Jesus say blessed are the merciful and not blessed are those who show grace?

Mercy is *not giving* someone what *they deserve*.

Grace is *giving* someone what they *do not deserve*.

For example, if someone steals a meal from the canteen, judgment will call out the wrongdoing and punish the crime. Conversely, mercy does not punish crime, while grace gives them another hot meal they do not deserve. You cannot show grace without a proper understanding of mercy.

IS MERCY A GIVEN?

Can we expect all people to be merciful to us? Nope. Mercy cannot be demanded or expected, nor are we entitled to it. We can only expect mercy from God, and even that is a gift we do not deserve! It is not my right to ask or expect mercy from people.

Does this mercy give a tit-for-tat? If I show mercy, will I be shown mercy in return? No! God's mercy would not be 'mercy' if given in response to our acts of mercy. It would be a wage. That would contradict the gospel, which says salvation is based on grace alone (Eph 2:8-9, Rom 11:6).

A WARNING!

Mercy is not treating a person as they might rightfully deserve. It is like the parable of the unmerciful servant (Matt 8:21-35). His debts were forgiven, while another servant owed him money. Technically, he had every right to throw his debtor in jail. He was shown a better way to handle it. The debt he could never repay was forgiven, and he had an opportunity to do the same but chose not to.

By contrast, in Matthew 26, another person was also shown mercy and was forgiven much. This person broke an alabaster jar at Jesus' feet in response to the mercy received.

We should have experienced the wrath and judgement of God; we are objects of mercy. Since we have been shown such mercy, we should respond compassionately when we encounter people's brokenness and make every effort to extend grace. This is especially true if it is someone who has ill-treated us. That is true mercy.[7] It is kindness and compassion in action. It starts in our homes. Are we caring, supportive, kind and giving at home? Are you kind to your co-workers where the environment may be unpleasant?

MERCY IS COSTLY

Mercy will cost you financially, emotionally, and in every other way. It is to give someone something they do not deserve, especially when they have hurt you. Jesus is not interested in our religious acts. He said, *"I desire mercy and not sacrifice." (Matt 9:13)*. You can pray, tithe, attend meetings, and still harbour unmerciful thoughts towards people. That is what Jesus was getting at when the law teacher asked Him what he should do to inherit eternal life. Jesus did not commend his religious acts. He told him the story of the Good Samaritan, who showed kindness and mercy toward the Jew who considered him unclean because of his ethnicity. Can we engage in love in action rather than just lip service to God?

Jesus is our Good Samaritan. Like the Samaritan in the parable, He despised and rejected us and gave His very life to save us and bind up the wounds inflicted upon us by a broken world.

WHAT MERCY IS NOT

We cannot give mercy where we are not authorised to. As a teacher, I must grade a student in all fairness. It is not up to me to overlook the wrong answers, mark them right, and call it mercy.

Mercy does not excuse wrongdoing. It is not re-labelling wrong as right. Remember, Jesus, in His mercy, did not condemn the woman caught in adultery, but neither did he condone her sin. He told her to go and sin no more. He called her up to a higher standard.

Mercy is not avoiding confrontation. Sometimes, we disguise our need to people-please as an act of mercy when we avoid conflict out of fear.

Mercy does not encourage dishonesty or disloyalty, nor does it condone indiscipline. It does not excuse irresponsibility or uncharitable behaviour under the guise of being merciful. Mercy becomes toxic when it enables irresponsible behaviour.

THE DILEMMA

Life is complicated for the Christ-follower who wants to live out their faith in a sinful world. It is not black and white as some might think. Though truth comes in layers and is multidimensional, it does not contradict itself. Sometimes, we must hold two truths in tension, like mercy and justice. We need to be merciful while not allowing God's standard of righteousness to slide. To do this, we need wisdom from above: *"But the wisdom that comes from heaven is first of all pure; then peace-loving, considerate, submissive, full of mercy and good fruit, impartial and sincere." James 3:17*

How would you answer these questions?

• Can a Christian be consistently merciful yet be a parent who disciplines an unruly child for disobedience?

• Can a Christian be consistently merciful and yet be an employer who pays good wages for excellent work but dismisses irresponsible employees who do shoddy work?

• Can a Christian be consistently merciful and yet be a legislator who enacts laws that give stiff penalties for drunk driving and child abuse?

• Can a Christian be consistently merciful yet be on a council of elders who follow the biblical mandate for church discipline and excommunicate a member for unrepentant, grievous sin?[8]

My answer to the questions is that I believe it is God's will that mercy and justice be mingled in all these spheres.

MINGLE MERCY AND JUSTICE

Micah 6:8 - "He has shown you, O man, what is good; And what does the Lord require of you? But to do justly, to love mercy, and to walk humbly with your God?"

God's will is that sometimes we deal with people as they deserve, whether punishment or reward (call that justice). God's will is also that sometimes we recompense people with something better than they deserve (call that mercy). In upholding the claims of justice, we bear witness to the truth that our God is a God of justice. In showing mercy, we witness the truth that our God is a God of mercy.

So, how do we know when to show mercy and when to show justice? This balance will come as we walk closer to Jesus. Sometimes, we may get it wrong and must trust our redeeming God to overturn our bad choices. Even in our execution of justice, we can show mercy. While we sometimes cannot condone a person's actions, we can still be gracious and loving in dealing with them.

KEY TURNING POINTS

- Remind yourself of how merciful God has been to you.
- Remind yourself of how people have been merciful to you.
- How can you make being merciful a lifestyle?Think about one way you can show mercy at work, at home and among friends.
- If we want to be more like Jesus, we must avoid the desire to be unmerciful. What can you remind yourself of when you are faced with that choice?
- Understand the difference between mercy, justice and grace. The best way to do this is to think of the real scenarios you have been in and re-write how each would play out if mercy, justice and grace were present.

REFLECTIONS

- Do you find it hard to be merciful?
- Can you think of times when you had to act justly, but you skipped being merciful? How would you handle this situation differently now?

ACTION PAGE
What knowledge can I rejoice in?

What is the Holy Spirit convicting me of?

What will I change in my beliefs, thougts and actions?

CHAPTER XII

THE PURE-HEARTED

"Blessed are the pure in heart, for they will see God."
Matthew 5:8

Being excluded from the Kingdom of God was a fear that every Jew carried. Nicodemus, a respected teacher, probably wrestled with this same question in his heart when he went to Jesus. Jesus responded by saying, *"Unless you are Born Again, you cannot see the Kingdom of God"* (John 3:3). Others, too, had asked similar questions, *"What shall I do to inherit eternal life?"* (Luke 10:25-28) The crux of these questions remains the same, "How can I be right with God?" The scriptures are clear. The standard is a pure heart.

You would have noticed that the beatitudes are progressing, which is the pinnacle. In practising the previously mentioned beatitudes, our hearts go through the refiner's fire and come out *pure*. The *pure in heart* will display the other five characteristics in the Beatitudes.

This chapter on the pure-hearted is longer than the rest because it lies at the core of the Beatitudes. We will dive deeper into this one and meditate on it for longer than the rest.

THE PHARISAICAL HEART

The Pharisees and another group called the Sadducees added hundreds of laws not mentioned in the Torah. The laws they put on the Jews were hard and heavy. It was a heartless, crushing yoke. Jesus came to disrupt their self-inputted theology and understanding of the scriptures.

I want to correct myself here. So far, we have talked about Jesus ushering in the Upside-Down Kingdom, but I propose that Jesus was introducing a *Right Side Up* Kingdom. The world toppled on its head when sin spun it out of control. Jesus came to restore all things to their original intent and design, turning them *Right Side Up!* The human interpretation made the law appear graceless, judging and shaming, but is that true of who God is? Did God shame King David? God always acted justly, and even in that, there was mercy. This beatitude hits hard at the gut of the Pharisees' insistence on their interpretation of law-keeping. You cannot understand God's commands without a relationship of love with Him. As I said earlier without a relationship with God, it gets reduced to rules. We know that God has always been interested in our hearts. Actions are judged based on the intentions of the heart.

Reflecting on this, I realise that God continuously revealed His interest in inner purity and that the Pharisees should have caught it. Did not God say, *"People look at the outward appearance, but the Lord looks at the heart."*? (1 Sam 16:7) Does Samuel not remind Saul that *"To obey is better than sacrifice"* (1 Sam 15:22)? In Joel, does he not remind His people to *"Rend your hearts and not your garments"* (Joel 2:13)? Jesus said, *"First clean the inside of the cup and dish, and then the outside also will be clean."* (Matt 23:26). What comes out of the mouth is more important than what goes in, *"For the mouth speaks what the heart is full of."* (Matt 12:34-40)

This is the heart of Christian life. Now more than ever, as Christ's followers, we are being called to a higher ground to live from a pure heart. We need passion to preserve and guard our hearts from being corrupted.

WHAT IS THE HEART?

It is the seat of all our emotions, affections, and desires – the centre of our beings. God always looks at the heart (*1 Sam. 16:7*), for out of the heart flows the issues of life. (*Prov. 4:23*) God is interested in Inner attitude, not outer actions. The heart is where good and evil stem from. *"Out of the heart come evil thoughts - murder, adultery, fornication, theft, and false witness." (Matt. 15:19)*. The Psalms say, *"The one with clean hands and a pure heart."* shall ascend the hill of the Lord. In Psalms 51, David's prayer was for a pure heart, for he knew the root of his sin and sinful actions.

WHO CAN HAVE A PURE HEART?

To start with, to cultivate a pure heart, one must first acknowledge its impure state. When we accept Jesus as our Saviour our sinful nature is crucified on the Cross. Through Christ, we have been justified and declared righteous. We all know that the gospel is about God's love, grace and forgiveness. However, it does not stop there. Yes, the gospel is about saving grace, and it is also that same grace that teaches us to say no to sin and yes to godliness (1 Tit 2:11-12).

God is continually cleansing us by *"washing us with the Word"* (Eph 5:26). The root word for clean (*Katharoi*) is also found in these contexts:

Jesus answered, "Those who have had a bath need only to wash their feet; their whole body is clean. And you are clean, though not every one of you." (John 13:10)

"You are already clean because of the word I have spoken to you." (John 15:3)

The words pure and clean carry the same weight and meaning. John 15:3 talks of an ongoing cleansing work within us. The chapter speaks of 'pruning,' understood as being purified or cleansed by faith. We are 'being sanctified'; we must first recognise the impurities in our hearts because you cannot fix what you do not recognise as broken.

We all carry the baggage of sinful habits. We must believe in the power of the finished work of the Cross to put them to death. Only when we acknowledge our hearts' need for constant cleaning and our mind's constant renewal do we position ourselves to see God.

WHAT IS A PURE HEART?

Another word for pure is *sincere* – without duplicity, agendas, manipulation, or double-mindedness. We must learn to walk to this degree of purity of heart. In those days, the artisan labelled well-made pots without cracks as 'Sincerus'. The product was therefore called *sincerus* in Latin from the words 'sine = without' and 'cera = wax' from which we get the English word 'sincere'. The cracks in the pots were fixed or hidden by filling them with wax; therefore, they were 'insincere'.

"Purity of heart is to will one thing."
Soren Kierkegaard.

The purity of the heart is single-mindedness. It is being pure in our desires.: It is when we choose to long for purity and hate impurity. It is when we are no longer conflicted about our desires or how we live our lives. James talks about us not being double-minded or having our affections and desires divided (*James 1:8*). James 4:8 says, *"Purify your hearts, you who are double-minded."* John Bunyan has a character in Pilgrim's Progress called *"Mr. Facing Both Ways."* which refers to being double-minded. When you are double-minded, you are not blessed.

A pure heart upholds the truth. It does not alter the truth at its convenience. The pure heart will seek truth and purity above self-preservation, knowing that purity comes at a price.

Being pure-hearted is being focused. Love the Lord your God with all your heart, mind, soul, and strength. Deny yourself daily and follow Jesus. Paul encourages us to run with focus as one who runs to win the crown (1 Cor. 9:24-27).

Purity of heart does not mean we will not sin or be without sin, for *"If we claim to be without sin, we deceive ourselves and the truth is not in us." (1 John 1:8)*. We are like gold, which has impurities that need to be refined in God's furnace of sanctification. It is a process of daily renewal every Christ follower goes through.

WHAT CORRUPTS OR DEFILES OUR HEARTS?

We are warned that in the last days, the hearts of many will grow cold. Is that not a sign of it becoming corrupted and impure? Galatians describes a heart that is cold towards God.
"The *acts of the flesh are obvious: sexual, immorality, impurity, and debauchery; idolatry and witchcraft; hatred, discord, jealousy, fits of rage, selfish ambition, dissensions, factions and envy; drunkenness, orgies, and the like. I warn you, as I did before, that those who live like this will not inherit the kingdom of God. But the fruit of the Spirit is love, joy, peace, forbearance, kindness, goodness, faithfulness,gentleness, and self-control. Against such things, there is no law. Those who belong to Christ Jesus have crucified the flesh with its passions and desires. Since we live by the Spirit, let us keep in step with the Spirit."*
Galatians 5:19-25

- **A hard heart** – when our hearts are clogged with pride, bitterness, judgement, unforgiveness, etc., it can dull the conscience.
- **A double-minded heart** –has its feet in two boats. When the going gets tough, it compromises with the truth. Jesus put it

another way – no one can serve two masters. (Matthew 6:24)

- **An unforgiving heart**. Unforgiveness clouds our vision, blocks our ears, and dulls our senses, and we cannot fully experience God's presence.
- **A proud heart**. Moses was the meekest man that lived, and he saw the face of God and lived! A proud heart will not admit wrong; therefore, it will not seek after righteousness and will lack humility.

THE PRICE OF A PURE HEART

How can we keep our hearts pure?

Ps 119:9, "How can a young person stay on the path of purity? By living according to your word."

We produce good fruit when we abide in Jesus and learn to walk in step with the Holy Spirit (John 15). Purity of the heart demands unwavering conviction, where you do not allow even a hint of conscious deceit. It means resisting manipulating situations, conversations, or people to get what you want. It refuses to deal with half-truths, cover-up lies and dishonesty. Those of us who are used to behaving this way will often struggle to discern the will and heart of God. Making good decisions has become difficult because the heart is clouded with mixed motives and agendas. James says, *"Such a person is double-minded and unstable in all they do." (James 1:7-8)*. If you are wearily nodding to these descriptions, I encourage you to hold up the mirror, the Word of God, to your soul daily. This daily reflection will prevent your conscience from being dulled, misinformed, or seared. Are you willing to let go of the need for self-preservation and humble yourself before God?

> ***When the pain of staying the way you are is greater than the***
> ***pain of the process of pain, you will embrace change.***
> ***Danny Silk***

God seeks purity. When He comes with His winnowing fork, will you be the wheat or the chaff? Knowing this, King David prayed.

Psalm 51, "Create in me a pure heart, O God, and renew a steadfast spirit within me.Do not cast me from your presence or take your Holy Spirit from me. Restore to me the joy of your salvation and grant me a willing spirit to sustain me."

How badly do you want the fruit of godly living in your life? That determines if you will seek it no matter the cost, and that is why only the poor in spirit, the meek, the ones that hunger for righteousness, can have a pure heart.

'FOR THEY SHALL SEE GOD'

When we are single-minded about becoming Christlike, the reward is that we will see God. Everyone who loves God yearns to have deep communion with Him the way Adam and Eve enjoyed in their pure, sinless state. Their only love was God and to delight in His presence. Still, years after their fall, every culture witnesses a longing to know and see God.

In ignorance, people go about it the wrong way. Man has tried to get closer to God or to become one with Him, but has always wanted to do it in their own strength. Some have tried to isolate themselves from the world. Some have been attempting to beat evil out of themselves or pay penance. Moses, too, had one desire, to see God's glory." David longed to see God's face and dwell in His presence forever.

WHAT DOES IT MEAN TO "SEE GOD"?

To "see God" is to have a deeper revelation, intimacy, and relationship with God through which we will know His ways and will. Those who pursued and received this revelation were changed forever. Take, for example. Isaiah in the temple (Isaiah 6:5-8) and Saul on the road to Damascus (Acts 9). Once they saw God, they saw how much their lives needed Him.

WHY IS SEEING GOD SO IMPORTANT?

Without Jesus, we have no life. He has the words of eternal life. He is the source of living water which will quench our thirst once and for all! He is the source of our being, joy, and fruitfulness. He is the Light of Life! All this comes from abiding in Him and growing in intimacy with Him. We develop a pure heart when we hunger and thirst for righteousness. You cannot have one without the other. That is why we cannot study nor practise any Beatitude in isolation. They are all interconnected.

> *"Purity of heart refers to a heart that is undivided in its devotion to God. It is a call to inward sincerity and single-minded focus on God's will, not just outward religiosity. R.C Sproul"*

I feel challenged to live up to this standard: Inside and out are the same, and it is the Right side up!

THE PRIZE FOR A PURE HEART.

The *'pure in heart'* receives the most beautiful reward. They shall enjoy greater intimacy with God than they could have imagined. The polluting sins of greed, envy, lust, deceit, and lies have a *blinding* effect on a person, but the *pure in heart* will see God.

The pure in heart can see God in nature.

The pure in heart can see God in Scripture.

The pure in heart can see God in one another.

The pure in heart can see the grace of God in their lives.

The reward of an intimate relationship with God must become our most compelling motivation for purity, greater than a fear of getting caught or the consequences of our wrongs. Purity means owning up to the impurities in our hearts and sometimes confessing to those affected by our sins. Those who have had a revelation of God hunger for more of Him. *O taste and see that the Lord is good.* There is an invitation to come and taste, to come and drink from Him (Isaiah 55:1, John 7:37-39, Rev 22:17). The more you thirst after the presence of God, nothing else will satisfy. Everything else will taste insipid, rotten, and putrid. You cannot stomach what the world tries to feed you. There is so much to say about the presence of God and how beautiful, inviting, and attractive it is! I hope you, too, will join me in pursuing what I am finding life-giving.

KEY TURNING POINTS

- God is interested in matters of the heart and not behaviour modification.
- The heart is the seat of all our values, character and desires.
- We need to guard our hearts from getting defiled.
- There is a cost to keeping one's heart pure.
- The reward is getting a deeper understanding and revelation of God.

REFLECTIONS

- Have I compromised with the truth, distorted it for my gain, or covered my faults?
- Am I humble enough to admit I am wrong, or does pride keep me from cultivating a pure heart?
- Do I recognise patterns, habits and attitudes that could hinder me from developing a pure heart?

ACTION PAGE
What knowledge can I rejoice in?
What is the Holy Spirit convicting me of?
What will I change in my beliefs, thougts and actions?

CHAPTER XIII

THE PEACEMAKER

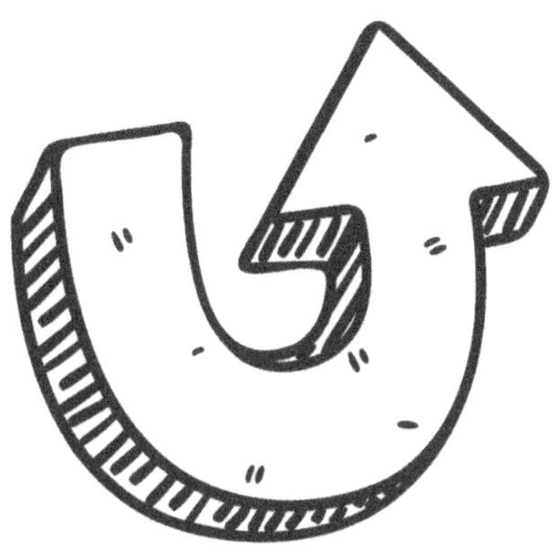

"Blessed are the peacemakers, for they will be called sons of God."
Matthew 5:9

As I was born in the 1960s, I have associated the word *peace* with the iconic peace stickers and popular slogans of the hippie movement, like "Make love, not war." You might also associate the word with a white flag declaring a truce or a surrender. *Peace* or *Shalom* was the common greeting among Jews, just like "Hello." Shalom is also a state of being.

SHALOM

Shalom in Greek is *Eirene*, which means "complete or whole". So, a rock that is *shalom* would have no cracks. A well-made brick wall with no gaps would be *shalom*.

When things are out of balance, it would be accurate to say that we do not have *shalom*. When we put things right, like our priorities, values, relationship with God, and relationship with one another, we are said to *have shalom*. This makes me stop to think about whether there is a lack of shalom in any area of my life. I can think of a few! Can you?

A PEACEFUL PEOPLE IN A PEACEFUL PLACE

Any guesses as to who and where this is? Shalom's first place on earth was the Garden of Eden. The first people who lived in Shalom were Adam and Eve. They were perfectly *whole*. They were complete and flourishing in their relationship with God, one another, and all creation. Nothing was out of sync. Everything was in perfect balance and harmony till sin came along, and shalom was destroyed. Life became fragmented and fractured in every area. That is why the Prince of Shalom needed to come to earth to restore His shalom and create a way for God to make peace with humanity and vice versa.

PEACE WITH GOD - AT A PRICE

We need peace *with* God to have the shalom or the peace of God. Everyone is searching for peace in their own way. Some people think they have found peace without God or through some kind of penance or meditation. We may enjoy temporary and partial peace without God; however, to have peace that lasts for eternity, we must have peace *with God*.

Humanism says that man is inherently good. Ever since shalom was broken by sin, man has been restless, "nasty, brutish and short" – Thomas Hobbes (Thomas was a clergyman who wrote a book in 1651). Modern-day philosophers criticise this assessment. I think his assessment is bang-on and lines up with the Bible. Read Romans 1 if you have any doubts. We are all capable of the vilest of sins, and our lives are short without a Saviour. It ends within 80-ish years, followed by eternal darkness and damnation, a place with zero shalom.

Humanity has been hostile towards God from the very beginning. Jesus, the first true peacemaker, came to restore shalom between God and man. He paid the price to bring shalom to us and reconcile man to God. So, peace comes first by *being* right with Godbefore we can even start *doing* anything.

Our Saviour's journey to Golgotha, marked with violence, hate and scorn, was the greatest journey to peacemaking we will ever know.

Jesus came to bring peace between God and man, without which we could not have become children of God.

Eph 2:13-14, *"But now in Christ Jesus, you who once were far away have been brought near by the blood of Christ. For he is our peace, who has made the two groups one and has destroyed the barrier, the dividing wall of hostility, by setting aside in his flesh the law with its commands and regulations. His purpose was to create in himself one new humanity out of the two, thus making peace."*

Romans 5:2:*"Therefore being justified by faith, we have peace with God through our Lord Jesus Christ."*

Jesus became that perfect sacrifice for the propitiation of our sins. The righteous, holy, sinless God must see justice through. Without that, there can be no shalom. His death on the cross restored the shalom between God and humanity. Peace is not just a relational condition between God and us, but Peace is a person. His name is Jesus, the Prince of Peace. He became our peace, i.e. he brokered peace between God and us. Then, He gives us Himself from where we begin to get restored to wholeness or Shalom.

Isaiah 53:5 *But he was pierced for our transgressions, he was crushed for our iniquities; the punishment that brought us peace was on him, and by his wounds, we are healed.*

"Peacemaking is like salt that makes the unpalatable palatable"
Charles Spurgeon.

To have the peace *of* God, we need to acknowledge Jesus' death on the cross and seek forgiveness for our sins. Only then will we live in peace *with* God. If you have never made peace with God by repenting of your sins and accepting Jesus' sacrifice on the Cross for them, today is a good day to do it.

THE MESSY PROCESS TOWARD PEACE

Let us not be fooled. The path to peacemaking can be rough and messy because we will deal with hurt, pain, misunderstandings, unkind words, and actions. As we know, these situations often do not get resolved quickly. Peacemaking involves moving towards trouble, intending to resolve conflict rather than walking away and burying it. We must run into the storm to come out on the other side of calm. If we run away, the storm will follow us and can overtake us.

Both parties must step down from their prideful positions and reach out to each other in humility, recognising their brokenness and neediness. The process can be very stormy. But when we put our confidence in the Prince of Peace and lay aside our pride, we can expect the storm to die through honest dialogue, humility, repentance and an earnest desire for reconciliation.

THE LASTING KIND!

Jesus came to bring a different kind of peace. John 12:27 says, *"Peace I leave with you; my peace I give you. I do not give to you as the world gives. Do not let your heart be troubled, and do not be afraid."*

We can trust in this peace because Jesus brought it to us. This peace is perfect; it is lasting and keeps us when we go through trials in our lives. It is a peace that sets a guard over our minds and hearts. Keeping our eyes on the Prince of Peace acts as a shield against anxiety and worry. Philippians 4:6-7 reminds us *"Do not be anxious about anything, but in every situation, by prayer and petition, with thanksgiving, present your requests to God. And the peace of God, which transcends all understanding, will guard your hearts and your minds in Christ Jesus."*

PIECE YOUR LIFE TOGETHER WITH PEACE

There is a false sense of peace we can get in escapism through sex, alcohol, drugs, gaming, etc. The truth is, we can never bring wholeness to our lives by ourselves. Jesus left us His peace. When we abide in Him, meditate on His word, and allow it to challenge us, we invite His shalom into our lives.

For some, this means forgiving yourself for what you feel you've messed up in your life and allowing God to heal those broken places. God gives beauty for ashes and wholeness to a fractured life.

MAKE PEACE, NOT WAR!

Paul starts most of his letters with a familiar salutation: "Grace and peace." Another critical factor in enjoying Shalom is true biblical fellowship. It is only when we have experienced God's grace that we also know God's shalom. In Jesus, the longed-for Shalom is found and experienced. It keeps us secure amidst any political, financial, or personal turmoil. You can experience Shalom despite the chaos around you.

Peace with others is central to the gospel because we seek forgiveness for our sins as we forgive others who sin against us. We make peace with God as we make peace with others. The second half of the Ten Commandments is about how we relate to others just as is the second half of the Beatitudes.

Peace with others is not an add-on but central to the message of Jesus. I have often heard of people being so 'happy and at peace in their relationship with God' but unable to stand the church. It is a contradiction of terms. "*If anyone says, I love God and hates (detests, abominates) his brother [in Christ], he is a liar; for he who does not love his brother, whom he has seen, cannot love God, Whom he has not seen.*" (1 John 4:20). As Christ's followers, making peace with our fellow humans, especially our brothers and sisters, is not an option.

PEACEMAKERS NOT KEEPERS!

Keeping the peace is typically where one would find themselves holding two feuding parties at arm's length of each other, hoping to stop all conflict. It's a band-aid solution that only prevents violence, but the real issues remain unresolved as ever.

Peacemaking is more of a lasting resolution. When we become children of God, we get His DNA, we become peacemakers. Not seeking revenge separates the Christ-follower from others who, in today's terms, will 'ghost' you to *keep the peace* because they do not dare face a peacemaking conversation.

"Blessed are the peacemakers, for they will be called children of God". Matt 5:9

Peace is not the absence of conflict but a proactive intervention that brings reconciliation between two parties. Jesus says that the blessed are the peacemakers and not peacekeepers. Making peace is messy and involves taking action. Peacemakers have difficult conversations and bring about restoration. We are Christ's ambassadors who are also called Ministers of reconciliation.

"So, peace takes a lot of work because it's not just the absence of conflict. True peace requires taking what's broken and restoring it to wholeness, whether it's in our lives, our relationships, or in our world. And that's the rich biblical concept of peace."
Bible Project

Peace with God and within yourself is within your volition or choice. Peace-making, however, is the most challenging part because it depends on how the other person responds. That is why Paul encourages us in *Romans 12:18: "If possible, so far as it depends on you, live peaceably with all."*

I remember a prayer of St Francis that goes -
Make me a channel of your peace.
Where there is hatred, let me bring your love.
Where there is injury, your pardon, Lord
And where there is doubt, true faith in You.

PEACE LIKE A RIVER

Since Peace is a person, Jesus; we have Him with us 24/7. Shalom has a residence in our hearts and we need to keep our minds fixed on Him.

Isaiah 26:3, "You will keep in perfect peace those whose minds are steadfast because they trust in you."

Phil 4:6-7, "Do not be anxious about anything, but in every situation, by prayer and petition, with thanksgiving, present your requests to God. [7] And the peace of God, which transcends all understanding, will guard your hearts and your minds in Christ Jesus."

We need to take our minds off worrying thoughts, and replace them with thanksgiving and prayer. When we live out peace with God, within ourselves and with others, the Shalom or wholeness of God flows through us like a river, bringing life to everything it touches. We are those oaks of righteousness that abide on the banks of that life-giving river which becomes the healing of the nations.

AS FAR AS IT DEPENDS ON YOU

How many of us have been in situations where you have tried to talk to someone who is upset with you but doesn't want to do anything about it? I sure have. It has been one of church life and leadership's most painful and traumatic parts. People will often deny the existence of a problem or find blame in you or someone or something. Sometimes, we hold onto offence because it legitimises or justifies how we treat someone.

We cannot have peace if we hold onto unforgiveness. Matthew 18 commands us to discuss our concerns with our brother or sister.

If they disagree that there is a problem, and they continue to mistreat you (by not talking to you, gossiping about you or ill-treating you), you are to take another mature fellow brother or sister along to help mediate (not someone who will take your side).

If the person is still unwilling, ask a church leader to help you. It is a long process and usually takes a few weeks or months. People process what is going on in their hearts differently and at different paces. We need to show grace and give people the time to change (just as God is so patient with us).

Remember, your goal is you want your brother or sister to have shalom with you. Throughout this, we ought to be open to being shown how we could have caused this conflict, too. If all fails, depending on the problem, the leaders might intervene at your invitation. But as far as it depends on you, you have made every effort at reconciliation as Paul says in *Romans 12:18:If it is possible, as far as it depends on you, live at peace with everyone.*

So, while reconciliation is the first step, and the onus is on us, restoration is the second, and it might not always happen; sometimes, we need to recognise that and be at peace with a necessary ending.

SONS!

The Greek word used in the original text is *Yióç (huios)*, which means a son. Before we get all hot under our collars about women being called sons, remember that men are also the Bride of Christ.

The cultural context of its time carries the significance of being called a 'son,' and that is the point here, not any gender bias. A son and his father share a similar nature.

In 1 A.D., as was the practice, sons were the legal heirs to their father's property. An adult son enjoyed many rights and privileges in a household compared to the women or the slaves. This is the point Jesus is making.

When we display His nature in handling peace, we truly resemble Him just as a son would his father.

So, whether male or female, we all get to share in His inheritance when we have been adopted into Jesus' family, as we are so beautifully reminded in Romans 8:17: *"Now if we are children, then we are heirs—heirs of God and co-heirs with Christ."*

PEACE ON EARTH

The angels announced the Messiah's birth with a proclamation of 'Peace on earth.' Indeed, Shalom left His heavenly abode to live in a broken world. When we become Christ's followers, we become ambassadors of peace. We have the authority and power to restore shalom to society, bringing healing to every broken area and bringing the right order to every aspect of it. So, we can help restore marriages and families, see unity between different classes, ensure that commerce flourishes for all, ensure equality, and remove oppression, exploitation, and injustice.

WHAT IS OUR RESPONSE?

Let us live in the joy and privilege of knowing the Prince of Peace as our personal Saviour.

Col 3:15 - *Let the peace of Christ rule in your hearts, since as members of one body, you were called to peace. And be thankful.*

Eph4:3*Make every effort to keep the unity of the Spirit through the bond of peace.*

Isaiah 52:7*How beautiful on the mountains are the feet of those who bring good news, who proclaim peace, who bring good tidings, who proclaim salvation, who say to Zion, "Your God reigns!"*

The Gospel's message is about Shalom and restoring wholeness to a broken humanity. Remember that we are both objects of God's love and renewal and God's agents of love and renewal. We are now agents of Shalom in a fractured world. When I think about it deeply and map out the biblical meaning of the word, I realise that Shalom is bigger than I thought. It is multi-dimensional and has so much to offer us and the world.

As I close my reflections on this Beatitude, I recall many areas in my life that need Jesus's shalom, and I am reminded not to shrink back from opportunities to be a peacemaker. The church and the world need more shalom than we can imagine. Studying the progression of the Beatitudes has made me realise that only the pure in heart can make peace because it means one must act justly, show mercy, and walk humbly before God even if it means it will cost you.

KEY TURNING POINTS

- Shalom is wholeness or completeness in every aspect of our lives.
- Our peace with God came at a price: Jesus' blood.
- Peacekeeping is easy. Peacemaking is messy but lasting.
- Our mandate is to bring peace on earth by helping people reconcile to God.

REFLECTIONS

- Do I recognise areas in my life that do not enjoy the shalom of God? What am I doing about it?
- Am I a peacemaker or a peacekeeper?
- Do I have the courage to be a peacemaker instead of a peacekeeper?

ACTION PAGE
What knowledge can I rejoice in?
What is the Holy Spirit convicting me of?
What will I change in my beliefs, thougts and actions?

CHAPTER XIV

THE PERSECUTED

"Blessed are those who are persecuted because of righteousness, for theirs is the kingdom of heaven."
Matthew 5:10

The Sermon on the Mount starts with the Beatitudes, proclaiming blessings to all who want to be in God's Kingdom. The Old Testament ended with curses, while the New Testament opens with Blessings. So, let us dive into the final verse of the Beatitudes.

Remember, we said the Beatitudes could not be understood or practised in isolation. They build upon one another. We first need to be *poor in spirit*, recognising our spiritual bankruptcy, which makes us *mourn* our condition, making us *meek* and humble. Our humility lets us realise that we must *hunger and thirst* for His Kingdom's righteousness. We can grant *mercy* to others from that place because we have received it first. Those who seek righteousness will cultivate a *pure heart* and want to bring *peace* in every situation. However, the result of living like this has consequences we may not like!

BLESSED ARE THOSE WHO ARE PERSECUTED BECAUSE OF RIGHTEOUSNESS

True happiness, God's blessings, and favour come from living in the right relationship with Him and with people. We are truly blessed when we fulfil God's law by loving Him and one another.

The first seven beatitudes are about living out the Kingdom's culture. The last one tells of what will happen to you when you want to be Christ-like!!! Any takers? If we live up to the first seven, the eighth will follow. Let me say this: we do not go seeking to be prosecuted. There is no virtue in doing that. Being persecuted is not something to ever wish for. However, should we ever be challenged by it, will we give up the standard of Kingdom culture to avoid being persecuted

IT IS NOT PERSECUTION

We are not blessed if we act unwisely, even if it is a Christian practice. For example, as Christ's followers, we do not bow to images, but that does not give us the right to go into someone's home and tell them to take their images down. We are to be wise as serpents and innocent as doves. Instead, we must be ready to answer everyone who asks us why we believe what we believe, but we must do this with discernment and respect, and our speech must be seasoned with salt (Col 4:6). Our deeds must speak more than our words. They will know we are disciples if we love one another (John 13:35). We must engage in acts of mercy without expecting anything in return. Let your love provoke questions about the faith you have and the hope you enjoy.

- If our language is offensive toward other people's faith, and they react, it is not persecution. We must not argue or criticise another person's beliefs. Even Paul showed empathy. In Acts, when he saw many idols in a city and commended them for their desire to know God (Acts 17:22-23).

- If we force people to do things against their convictions and they turn against us, it is not persecution. Instead, pray for them and point them to scripture when they ask you questions. Do not force people to give up religious icons of their previous faith or take off any symbols they wear until *they* are convinced it is something they need to do. Wait for the Holy Spirit to work in their hearts, just as He has in yours.

I remember a time when the family would get into arguments over faith. Birthday parties would become moments filled with tension, heated arguments, flying, and raised tempers. The result is that not one person was attracted to the gospel through that. Instead, it led to strained relationships. We had to repent our insensitive ways, and those relationships took a few years to heal. I realised that no one can be won to heaven through a clever debate. Salvation is the work of the Holy Spirit and Him alone.

- When we provoke the authorities by being brash or obnoxious, and they retaliate, it is not persecution. The churches in China and South Korea survived and flourished because they learned to be wise as serpents. Do not attract unnecessary attention to yourself. There is a fine line between wisdom and presumption, wisdom and fear. We need to become all things to all men while presenting an unchanging gospel. We present a timeless gospel while keeping in step with the culture and times without compromise. That requires wisdom from above.

If you live the beatitudes right, trust me, you will face real persecution. Why? How could living a good life attract brickbats? Precisely for that reason. Light and darkness have nothing in common. We come from not only two different but also opposing kingdoms. Our new nature in Christ is offensive, and a stench in the nostrils of some. You will not be able to avoid some wrongful accusations and criticisms.

Here are some things the early Christians were accused of:

- Cannibalism - A Gross and deliberate misrepresentation of the practice of the Lord's Supper was spun into a case of cannibalism.
- Immorality—The weekly "Love Feast" and private gatherings for meals and sharing resources were maliciously labelled as places for promiscuity.
- Revolutionary fanaticism - Due to the belief that Jesus would return and bring an apocalyptic end to history.
- Splitting families - When one marriage partner or parent became a Christian, their conversion often caused division in the family; this was weaponised against the church.
- Treason - The early Christians would not honour the Roman gods and participate in emperor worship; this landed them accusations of treason.[1]

Paul warned in *2 Timothy 3:12*, *"All who desire to live godly in Christ Jesus will be persecuted."* Peter told his readers, in 1 Pet 4:12, *"Do not be surprised at the fiery ordeal among you . . . as though some strange things were happening to you"*. James was similarly blunt about the inevitability of trials.[2].

John 15:18-19 "If the world hates you, you know that it hated Me before it hated you. If you were of the world, the world would love its own; but because you are not of the world, but I chose you out of it, the world hates you". Jesus is talking about being persecuted because of Him, i.e. When we live like Him and do what He tells us to do.

WHAT IS RIGHTEOUS LIVING?

True righteousness is not practised for its own sake, i.e. to make ourselves look good or where we self-righteously take the higher moral ground. It is practised for Jesus's sake.

The mercy, purity, and peacemaking of a disciple of Jesus comes from abiding in Jesus (*John 15:15: "Without me, you can do nothing."*) and is done for the honour of Jesus. It is this attachment to Jesus that gives our righteousness its distinct character.[3] It is living according to the Word of God.

As I think about this, I realise there is a difference between being self-righteous and righteous for Christ's sake. Self-righteousness is when we believe we are right and want to defend our convictions. We could very well be on the morally correct side, but we are defending our stand because it is precisely that – *our* stand and not for the sake of Christ.

Righteousness, for Christ's sake, is the qualifier. Not every moral person who is persecuted is blessed in the manner the Beatitudes speak of. Righteousness, for Christ's sake, may sometimes mean letting go of your ego or the issue because love is the greater good. We must persistently walk in step with the Holy Spirit and abide in His Word to understand the will of the Lord. Putting the Beatitudes into practice is not easy. We must love our enemy, pray for those who hate us, and bless those who curse us. It is countercultural. The Kingdom of God is not about entitlement but about laying down our lives.

WHAT DOES PERSECUTION LOOK LIKE IN OUR DAILY LIVES?

Each of us faces different challenges. Not everyone is called to be a martyr or to go to jail. Nevertheless, our convictions will be challenged daily. Our small daily steps of living the faith will help us grow strong in our convictions. I am reminded of the verse in Jeremiah 12:5: *"If you have run with men on foot and they have made you tired, then how can you run as fast as horses?"*

Here are some Places where we could be challenged:

At work: It may mean going to work or logging in on time. It may be doing what is asked without fudging anything, even if team members are pressuring you to do it. They may try to guilt trip you, saying things like, "Because of you, we will all get a bad rating", etc. How would you handle it?

Your stand to live righteously can be challenged when you are asked to tell *white lies* to cover up missed deadlines. These are areas of righteous living for which no one will pat you on the back.

You might be isolated when colleagues or friends exclude you from social gatherings because your presence pricks their consciences about their choices.

Your boss may have it in for you when you want to establish a work-life balance and log off so you can spend time with your family. As a result, you are denied a promotion despite faithfully completing your work.

In the family: You could face challenges among family who taunt you for your faith or threaten to disown you.

Your stand to refuse to marry a non-Christian could be challenged by your family, putting pressure on you to compromise your beliefs for their satisfaction.

In the neighbourhood: Maybe you do not agree with some questionable decisions taken by your apartment block Committee, and they start to slander and oust you.

I have faced some of the above, and it was not easy.

TWO RESPONSES TO RIGHTEOUS LIVING

What would anyone have against a meek person or against someone who shows mercy or a peacemaker? It simply does not make sense.

Righteous living can invoke curiosity about our hope or provoke persecution. The latter is usually because people feel pricked by their guilt and blame you for making them feel like they do.

If you live for the praises of men, you will die by their criticism.

People love their evil lifestyle and choices, and they need to be able to justify it. They demonise you because unless they do that, their hatred toward you is not fair.

One of the causes of persecution is that those who do not follow Christ have no stomach for godly righteousness. You will be persecuted for your faith, and you will be called a bigot and narrow-minded. When you stand up for godly lifestyle choices, viz. that you believe in purity before marriage, faithfulness in marriage, or how you choose to raise your children, you will be mocked and criticised as being too religious and old-fashioned.

As a church leader, you could face this when confronting sin in people's lives. People will lash out at you and spread false rumours. They will twist the narrative to suit their version of the story. You will want to explain yourself to people, but instead, you need to entrust yourself to God, who sees all things. Do not expect everyone to applaud your stand. You did not do it for them.

Have you been persecuted for righteousness's sake? If people have never noticed that you are different, self-examination is necessary. We are in this world, but not for its values and systems.

If the world has got into you, where you are living a life of compromise, and you justify it by misusing the word "grace", you need to repent of doing that. Grace empowers you to live God's way and not to excuse or condone our wrongs. Jesus said a lukewarm Christian would be spewed out of His mouth. We do not precisely know what that means; whatever it is, you do not want to be in that place!

God has given us His Holy Spirit to strengthen, encourage, comfort, guide, and lead us into all truth. The Holy Spirit is the divine power that gives us the strength to say no to sin and yes to godly choices.

Here are some examples of people who lived righteous and faced persecution.

- Abel was killed by his own brother.
- David was hunted down by Saul.
- Uriah was murdered at David's hand.
- Elijah was hounded by Jezebel.
- Daniel and his friends received and faced death threats.

- All but one of the apostles all died as martyrs.
- The churches in China and elsewhere are still being persecuted for following Christ.

HOW SHOULD WE RESPOND TO PERSECUTION?

"For theirs is the Kingdom of heaven." Matt 5:10

Firstly, do not go seeking persecution. We are not ever told that it is of greater value to die a martyr's death or that we are better Christ-followers when we invite persecution. The next verse sayswe are blessed when people falsely accuse and persecute us. We must rejoice and be glad because we suffer the same fate as Jesus. No servant is greater than his Master. We must bless them, pray for them, and do good to them. Remind yourself that these troubles are there but for a while. (2 Cor 4:17). A crown awaits all those who persevere till the end. (Matt 5:12) We do not stand alone. We have thousands standing beside us, cheering us on. They are the great cloud of witnesses from Hebrews chapter twelve. The promise is that the Kingdom of Heaven has come here to the earth and will in the coming age.

There is persecution at the individual level and then at the larger level, such as the Church of Jesus. If you have been reading the news, you will see that the kind of persecution the early church faced is not unknown to us.

In my country, this is becoming a daily reality for some. Religious intolerance and hate propaganda are on the rise. Scores of churches are being attacked and vandalised; people are beaten up, killed or unlawfully put into jail on trumped-up charges. How shall we respond?

"It is not without significance that the disciples are to be known by their love, the world by its hatred."
Morris

Hate and retaliation are easy options, but it takes courage to continue loving and serving in the face of them. We can stand firm with love in our hearts against the tide of hate only when we are strengthened in God. We are asked to rejoice and be exceedingly glad because we have a reward in heaven waiting for us.

The Christian calling is a great one. It is the highest and the most challenging one you will ever have to live up to. You can chuck your job or change your career, city, or house, but this commitment is for life and the age to come. May we be counted as worthy, who will not look back or consider following Jesus too heavy a price to pay. This is a challenge for everyone who says they follow Christ, not just for church leaders or missionaries.

All of us have a Christian calling to glorify Jesus. *And if we are children, then we are heirs of God and fellow heirs with Christ, provided we suffer with him so that he may also glorify us. (Rom 8:17)* He is worthy of all our devotion, adoration, suffering, and sacrifice. May we not be found wanting, but may we come through every test as pure gold.

Kingdom culture is God's will for the world. We have been asked to pray, "Your kingdom come; Your will be done on earth as it is in heaven." It will happen when you and I internalise Kingdom values as our core beliefs and demonstrate them in our lives. Only then will we infuse our society with them like salt does the earth.

THE PROMISE

The Beatitudes start and end with the promise of the Kingdom of Heaven. This promise is given in the present tense. All the other beatitudes have a present action and future promise to them.

These promises are like bookends to the Beatitudes for the poor in spirit and persecuted. The "now and not yet" dimension of these promises rings loud for them. We receive them in part now, and there is more to obtain in the future.

KEY TURNING POINTS

- A Godly life will invite persecution.
- Do not be persecuted because you did not behave wisely.
- Our righteousness can be the aroma of Christ for some and a provocation to wickedness for others.
- We are promised the kingdom of heaven when we suffer for Christ.

REFLECTIONS

- Have you faced any persecution because of your faith in Jesus?
- Have you faced criticism because you did not handle yourself well while sharing your faith? What would you change now that you are aware?
- What does gospel contextualisation look like without compromising the truth in your cultural setting?

ACTION PAGE
What knowledge can I rejoice in?

What is the Holy Spirit convicting me of?

What will I change in my beliefs, thougts and actions?

CHAPTER XV

AGENTS OF CHANGE

Throughout this book, we have seen what it means to be poor in spirit, mourn, be meek, hunger and thirst for righteousness, be merciful, pure in heart, and be a peacemaker. How has this teaching challenged and changed you? Our meditation on the Beatitudes calls Christ's followers to march to a different drum. It contradicts and will not sync with what everyone else is marching to. It is a call to repent or turn from one way of belief and behaviour to the truth. Jesus' *Right-side Up* culture tells us what the Kingdom is like and what the King expects from His subjects. God never intended for our relationship with Him and one another to be one where we have many hurdles to jump. It was supposed to be without strife, an easy yoke, full of joy and pleasure, just as the Psalmists say, *"In your presence is fullness of joy and at your right-hand pleasures for evermore"*!

The last beatitude warns us that we will face persecution if we choose to live righteously. How, then, shall we live? The answer is in the verses that follow.

BEING VERSUS DOING

We are to live unobtrusively without drawing attention to ourselves yet influence everything around us. Like salt and light, powerful agents of change that work subtly but unmistakably, neither draw attention to themselves, yet they transform the atmosphere. It is about our presence and essence—*simply being*—rather than just doing. In this chapter, we will only mediate on us being compared to salt.

AGENTS OF CHANGE

In Matthew's gospel, Jesus tells us we are *the salt of the earth*. Luke 14:34-35 further explains what Jesus meant when He called us Salt. Those who originally heard this analogy did not picture a saltshaker like we do today. Luke shows us three uses of salt: in food, on the land, and in the dunghill!

SALT THE ENHANCER OR CATALYST

In Jesus' time, they got their salt from the Dead Sea, which comprises 27% salt. The salt they collected was not just a regular cooking salt but a combination of many salts, including Potassium Chloride or Potash. Potash is used as a fertiliser for plants. When Jesus calls us the salt of the Earth, He refers to fertiliser and not cooking salt contained in a shaker! We are meant to be fertilisers, catalysts that promote good growth.

SALT THE DESTROYER

The other use of salt that Jesus refers to is far removed from our life experience: the dunghill! It is not in a barn or a stable but somewhere in the outhouse or the backyard of people's homes. In those days there were no toilets or sanitation like we're used to. People did their business in a hole in the ground and covered it with mud and a handful of salt, a disinfectant.

Salt can enhance the growth of good things and prevent the growth of bad things. Those who first heard Jesus' comparison understood this perfectly because that is how they used salt daily.

Now, when you think about it, you will realise the reference was never a dainty sprinkling of salt. When salt is used as a fertiliser, a handful or a sack full might be needed to produce the desired harvest. Likewise, you would not gently sprinkle salt on the dunghill. Fists full of salt had to be used to prevent bacteria from spreading.

When comparing Christ's followers to salt in this manner, a small sprinkling is not enough. The proportion counts. For a long time, I thought of us as sprinkles of salt in a shaker resting on a dining table. However, that is not how Jesus called us to be salt. We cannot change the trajectory of the diminishing values of society unless we show up in significant numbers to boost an upward trend on our shoulders. We need to be significantly felt and heard to create an impact of magnitude.

SALT THE INFLUENCER

What percentage of the community do we need to be to trigger change? There are varying opinions on this; some say 10% while others say one needs to be 30% to be of critical mass, to be the tipping point to affect or change a trend or culture. Either way, I feel encouraged that we do not need to be in the majority to affect change. The minority mindset narrative that we are "too few or too small to make a change" holds no water. Remember, Jesus likened us to salt and not the vast crop in the field. He felt that comparison was and is enough to affect society's ecosystem. Therefore, the salt needs to be in the field or, in our case, our communities. Salt is useless if it is all stocked up in jars in a pantry! Salt sitting in the jars with other salt will not create any change. Our presence will be effective only when we actively engage the community outside of our churches.

SALT THE PRESERVER

As you will find out through this chapter, salt is undeniably important. Another way it was used in those days was as a preserver of meat. People would carry dried salted meat with them when they travelled on long journeys. Salt also preserves meat through the hard winter months, without which the meat would rot and go bad. Therefore, salt was used to prevent the meat from rotting.

So back to us being salt. We prevent moral decay in society when we are present and *effective*. There is a dual function of both preserving and destroying simultaneously, in that the meat is preserved and prevented from rotting. Society needs to be preserved and prevented from moral decline.

"Meat goes bad when there is not enough salt" – John Stott

Jesus saw isolation as a potential problem and reminded His disciples and us that we are in the world (in the earth as fertilizer) but not of the world. Somewhere in Christendom, we got it into our heads that if we are to stay morally and spiritually pure, we need to isolate and stay in our church silos huddled in with church programs, church schools and church community events. How wrong we have been! Is it any wonder that society has started to rot?

When you look at the Beatitudes and the rest of the Sermon on the Mount, it is all about our interaction with our neighbours and even with people who do not treat us right. Where does that happen? It happens as we engage with society around us. When we live out the standards of the *Right-Side-Up* culture, people might even try to imitate it because it is attractive. Is it not the reason why people flock to Christian-run schools because they are guaranteed a standard of education and some impartation of good morals?

Earlier, I emphasised the word *effective* because Jesus does point to the possibility of salt being ineffective! If we do not integrate with society, we cannot influence it. The best job is being salt where there is none, so you can be an agent of positive change and prevent corruption and decay.

SALTY SALT!

We often use quality and quantity in contrast, so how does that play out here? Jesus addressed that, too when He refers to salt losing its saltiness! Can salt become unsalty? If you mix salt with another substance that looks like it but does not have its properties, you will notice that its effect has weakened.

In the same way, if our lives are compromised and our values diluted, we will cease to be effective change agents in our community. Do we, Christ's followers, stand out in society for the right reasons? At our place of work, do we have a reputation for being the most honest and conscientious? Do we have a reputation for purity where we do not indulge in sexually immoral behaviour? Are we honest with our money and paying taxes, giving Caesar what belongs to Caesar and God what belongs to Him? Are we good neighbours? Are we law-abiding citizens?

While many of our values are being challenged even by the laws of the land, will we hold onto our values, or will the church succumb? Will we try to be relevant and, in doing so, lose our distinctiveness as that city set on a hill? We must contend with these questions as the world takes on a fluid understanding of truth and morals.

Jesus asks, "Can it be made salty again?" The answer is no! What does this mean for a Christ follower? It means we get rid of all the compromises and start afresh completely. A compromising

Christian is ineffective for the kingdom and cannot be used by God to impact society.

A SALTY LIFE

Salt, as a tastemaker, brings out the flavours of the food. Good things in our culture can become even better when salt is applied to it. Culture, when redeemed through the Cross, can become salty, meaning it can be restored to its original purpose and design, which is to be life-giving. For example, while the Arts, movies, commerce, and science have good elements, they are also flawed and dark in many ways. When we are salt, there will be love, justice, righteousness, peace, equality, the flourishing of every art, trade, industry, science, medicine and more, truly making the world heaven on earth! Living out the Beatitudes is what being salty is all about.

When we are salty, it will also provoke and challenge the evil in society. Be ready for persecution, hate and rejection. Jesus offers us comfort in Matt 5:12, reminding us that we will face the same trials as the prophets of old and will be rewarded in the age to come.

KEY TURNING POINTS

- As salt, we are called not to stay in a saltshaker but to be scattered in society.
- We are called to be catalysts for change.
- We are called to preserve a good ecosystem.
- We need to challenge what is ungodly to prevent rot in society.
- To be salty, we need to live uncompromised lives.
- As salt let us not stay stuck in our silos called church, and as light let us not duck for cover when we can bring the wisdom of God to bear on society.

REFLECTIONS

- Do I isolate or relate with society?
- How has my presence been a catalyst, preserver or provocation to evil?
- Am I a salty Christ-follower?

ACTION PAGE

What knowledge can I rejoice in?

What is the Holy Spirit convicting me of?

What will I change in my beliefs, thougts and actions?

CHAPTER XVI

WHERE DO WE GO FROM HERE?

While meditating and studying the Beatitudes, one could be inspired, challenged, or overwhelmed. The latter is not the feeling I want to leave you with. At this point, it will be good to remind ourselves that the Beatitudes were given to those who wanted to be a part of Jesus' Kingdom.

WHY PRACTICE THE BEATITUDES?

It is the foundation for Christian living. Everything hinges on this. Jesus, a few hours before His arrest, tells the disciples they should live by adopting a poverty of spirit that says, "Apart from you, Lord, I can do nothing" (John 15:5)

Kingdom lifestyle is the best evangelistic tool you will ever find. By demonstrating Christ-like love to one another, all men shall know we are His disciples.

If we were to put the practices of the Beatitudes into a matrix, it would look a little like this -

	LOVE	FORGIVING	DYING TO SELF
LOVE	Nurturing	Reconciliation	Sacrifice
FORGIVING	Compassion	Healing	Selflessness
DYING TO SELF	Total Surrender	Letting go.	Transformation

The Matrix

In this matrix, each cell represents a combination of two concepts and suggests the resulting outcome or characteristic. Here is a description of each combination:

- **Nurturing:** Love manifests as care and support that provides nourishment and growth to those around us.
- **Reconciliation:** Love and forgiveness work together to mend broken relationships and restore harmony.
- **Sacrifice:** Love and dying to self-involve, giving up one's desires or interests for the benefit of others.
- **Compassion:** Forgiveness, when accompanied by deep empathy, makes room for us to understand the one who caused harm.

- **Healing:** Forgiveness makes room for restoring emotional well-being, lightens the load we carry and carries the potential for healing wounds.
- **Selflessness:** The act of forgiving requires setting aside personal ego and focusing on the well-being of others.
- **Total Surrender:** Dying to self is an act of complete surrender and submission. It is choosing to love God and those around us, allowing that to guide every aspect of our lives.
- **Letting go:** You cannot die Dying to self cannot exist parallel with if there are attachments that weigh you down, like grievances or the need for retribution. With true forgiveness and self-forgetfulness, we can let go of the past.
- **Transformation:** Dying to self leads to a profound inner change, shaping and renewing us into more compassionate, selfless, and loving individuals.

CONDUCT OR CHARACTER

Jesus did not come to create a code of conduct for us to follow. Every society has a code of conduct, but none have addressed the heart. Reducing the Beatitudes to a moral code would be a tragedy. You will see that the Beatitudes cannot be lived in our own strength. If we try to, we become like the Pharisees who reduced God's Law to rigid rules.

If we do not start by being poor in spirit, we will never acknowledge our need for a Saviour, and we will never be able to live out these values. In John 3, Jesus tells Nicodemus, a Pharisee, that *"unless a man is born again, he cannot enter the Kingdom of God!"* It is such a radical statement in so many ways. In one sweeping statement, the old era of being a 'chosen people' by birth was replaced with a free and open choice to be His people. Tradition or ancestry is not the doorway; it is through repentance and becoming poor in spirit that one receives the Kingdom.

Paul echoes the same truth in Ephesians 2:8-10: *For it is by grace you have been saved, through faith—and this is not from yourselves, it is the gift of God— not by works so that no one can boast.For we are God's handiwork, created in Christ Jesus to do good works, which God prepared in advance for us to do.*

Then Paul goes on to explain in verses 11 to 13 of the same chapter, saying: *Therefore, remember that formerly you who are Gentiles by birth and called "uncircumcised" by those who call themselves "the circumcision" (which is done in the body by human hands)— remember that at that time you were separate from Christ, excluded from citizenship in Israel and foreigners to the covenants of the promise, without hope and without God in the world.But now in Christ Jesus, you who once were far away have been brought near by the blood of Christ.*

This is critical to understanding and applying The Beatitudes and Sermon on the Mount. Jesus tells His disciples in Matt 11:28-30 that while the yoke put on the people by the Pharisees was heavy, His yoke is light. It means that Jesus wants us to relate to the Law without it feeling heavy and that there is a way to do that, His way. What is His way? Jesus fulfilled the Law through relationships and not rituals. That is why He invites us to abide in Him, to live under the power of the Holy Spirit (Acts 1:8)

The only way to live the Christian life is to have a spirit of humility that recognises the need for a Saviour every moment of every day. Only as we learn to abide in Him will we produce good, lasting fruit. Jesus reminds us that His grace is sufficient, and His power fulfils the purpose for which it is poured out in our lives.

PEOPLE NEED LOVIN'

The second half of the Beatitudes can only be practised in a community. We cannot live this life isolated from the world. The Pharisees were righteous in keeping the letter of the Law down to every minute detail. However, Jesus challenged His hearers to supersede the righteousness of the Pharisees because, despite their strife for perfection, neglect was their duty toward their fellow humans. They had no love nor compassion. Thus, Jesus takes the Law to a new level in Matt 22:27-40.*Jesus replied: "'Love the Lord your God with all your heart and with all your soul and with all your mind.'This is the first and greatest commandment. And the second is like it: 'Love your neighbour as yourself.'All the Law and the Prophets hang on these two commandments."* The Greek word there for 'like' is ὁμοία (***homoia***), which means similar or of equal rank! Therefore, you cannot keep one and break the other. They are two sides of a coin.

The challenge to all of us today is obedience, not knowledge of the Bible. It is where my challenge began and continues. I will not get it right, I will make mistakes, and I know that one day, on the other side of death, all things will be perfect. While I live on this Earth, the goal of my salvation is that Christ be formed in me, not just for my sanctification and holiness but also for me to fulfil the apostolic mandate outlined in the Great Commission and Isaiah 61.

RIPPLE EFFECT

When the whole church lives out the whole gospel in the whole of society, we will become that city set on a hill that cannot be hidden. We will become the manifold wisdom of Christ on display, that chosen nation, a royal priesthood, and a people set apart that will put God's glory on display for the world to see. Living out the Beatitudes and the whole Sermon on the Mount is how to be truly human. As objects of God's ongoing renewal work in us, as we live as salt and light, we also become agents of change that will have an effect as we aim to bring the shalom of God to our villages, towns and the country in which we live thus fulfilling Habakkuk's prophecy of the Earth being filled with the knowledge of the glory of the Lord even as the waters cover the sea. I want to quote one of my all-time favourite poems, which is, in many ways, a reflection on the Sermon on the Mount.

IF - BY RUDYARD KIPLING (1865-1936)

If you can keep your head when all about you
Are losing theirs and blaming it on you;
If you can trust yourself when all men doubt you,
But make allowance for their doubting too;
If you can wait and not be tired by waiting,
Or, being lied about, don't deal in lies,
Or, being hated, don't give way to hating,
And yet don't look too good, nor talk too wise;

If you can dream—and not make dreams your master;
If you can think—and not make thoughts your aim;
If you can meet with triumph and disaster
And treat those two impostors just the same;
If you can bear to hear the truth you've spoken
Twisted by knaves to make a trap for fools,
Or watch the things you gave your life to broken,
And stoop and build 'em up with wornout tools;

If you can make one heap of all your winnings
And risk it on one turn of pitch-and-toss,
And lose, and start again at your beginnings
And never breathe a word about your loss;
If you can force your heart and nerve and sinew
To serve your turn long after they are gone,
And so hold on when there is nothing in you
Except the Will which says to them: "Hold on";

If you can talk with crowds and keep your virtue,
Or walk with kings—nor lose the common touch;
If neither foes nor loving friends can hurt you;
If all men count with you, but none too much;
If you can fill the unforgiving minute
With sixty seconds' worth of distance run—
Yours is the Earth and everything that's in it,
And—which is more—you'll be a Man, my son!

RING OUT THE OLD BRING IN THE NEW.

As I draw these reflections in the Beatitudes, let us remember that Jesus was ushering His Kingdom and showing us how to enter His Kingdom and how we ought to live. He starts with the call to repent or *turn* from the old ways of doing things. It was the dawn of a new Era. The old has gone; the new has come. Jesus taught His disciples how to be truly human, as God always intended. A change that required a hundred-and-eighty-degree *turn* was at hand. The Messiah had spoken.

Jesus came down from the mountain preaching the Kingdom of God and went about healing the sick, doing good and casting out demons. He continued to expound on the characteristics of the Kingdom of God through His teachings and the parables about the Kingdom. Jesus was reframing everything the Jews believed and practised. He was challenging everything they thought was righteous and acceptable to God. He turned it on its head when He said, "You have heard it said, but I say to you..." People marvelled at the authority with which he spoke.

Indeed, He was saying that the new way of looking at the Law and relating to God cannot be contained in the old structures. New wine needs new wineskins. What would that look like? For that, we must not stop our reflections on the Beatitudes but continue to dig deeper into the entire Sermon on the Mount. For now, let us put into practice what we have now become conscious of and *turn* from our old ways to embrace the new. Amen!

ACTION PAGE
What knowledge can I rejoice in?
What is the Holy Spirit convicting me of?
What will I change in my beliefs, thougts and actions?

References

BOOKS:

- Morgan, Christopher. "The Kingdom of God. (Vol. 4)" 2012.
- Pink A. W An Exposition of the Sermon on the Mount. 2013
- MountWright, N. T. Simply Christian: Why Christianity Makes Sense. 2006.
- Stott, John The Message of the Sermon on the Mount. 1978
- Strong's Exhaustive Concordance of the Bible. 1890
- Wright, N. T. The New Testament in Its World: An Introduction to the History, Literature, and Theology of the First Christians, 2019.

COMMENTARIES:

- Bible Hub: The Greek and Hebrew Lexicon and the Greek and Hebrew Interlinear Bible
- Matthew Henry. Commentary on the Whole Bible: Matthew.
- O'Donnell, Douglas. "Here and Now and Not Yet of the Beatitudes: Matthew 5 Commentary."
- Spurgeon, Charles. The Beatitudes: Sermon and Exposition.
- Guzik, David. Commentary on Matthew.

SERMONS, YOUTUBE VIDEOS, AND AUDIO CONTENT:

- BibleProject. "Why Is Jesus Always Talking About the Kingdom of God? Ep. 1." Youtube, 2022.
- BibleProject. "What Does It Mean to Join God's Kingdom? - Gospel of the Kingdom Ep. 3." Youtube, 2022.
- Ferguson, Sinclair. "The Beatitudes: Sermon on the Mount". Youtube, 2021

- Guzik, David. "Preaching the Kingdom: Matt 5:1-2." YouTube, 2019.
- Guzik, David. "Blessed Are the Peacemakers - Matt 5:9". Enduring Word, 2020.
- Hamrick, Gary. The Beatitudes. Cornerstone Chapel. Youtube, July 2020.
- Keller, Tim. "The Upside-Down Kingdom." Youtube, 2015.
- Keller, Tim. "The Inside Out Kingdom." The Mount: Life in the Kingdom, Youtube, 2019.
- Keller, Tim. "How to Be Changed by the Gospel: Part 1 & 2." Youtube, 2018.
- Mackie, Tim. "A Kingdom of Blessing [Matthew]." Youtube, 2017.
- Pawson, David. "The Kingdom of God."Youtube, 2018.
- Smith, Colin. "Blessed are the pure in heart (Matt 5:8)." Youtube, 2013
- Smith, Colin. "Cultivating Peace from Matthew 5:9". Youtube, 2013
- Spurgeon, Charles. "The Beatitudes (Sermon on the Mount) : Sermon and Exposition.|Matt 5:1-12 ". Youtube, 2023
- Sproul, R. C. The Beatitudes. Youtube, 2022
- Wright, N. T. "Messiah and the People of God. Youtube, 2020.
- Wright, N. T. "The New Testament in Its World: How History Can Revitalize Faith." YouTube, 2019.
- Pink, A. W. An Exposition of the Sermon on the Mount. Youtube, 2020

ONLINE RESOURCES:

- Bible Gateway - This is for all Bible references in the NIV translation.
- D'Cruz, Lasya. "Creating Counterculture: Part 7." Word of Grace Church, November 2021.
- Hebrew for Christians. "The Beatitudes."

- Smith, Ash. "Come Up Here." Catch the Fire
- Wright, N. T. "The Future of the World." Fuller Forum, 2014.
- Piper, John. "The Beatitude Series." Desiring God, 1986.
- Piper, John. "The Beatitudes and the Gospel of the Kingdom." Desiring God.
- The Gospel Coalition. "The Kingdom and the Church."
- Bible Hub - For the Greek and Hebrew Interlinear Bible
- WordOfGraceChurch: The Kingdom of God in the New Era. http://blog.wordofgracechurch.org/2022/08/the-kingdom-of-god-in-new-era.html
- WordOfGraceChurch: The Kingdom Of God. http://blog.wordofgracechurch.org/2021/05/the-kingdom-of-god.html

ARTICLES:

- "Journal of Biblical Counselling." Vol. 19, No. 2 (Winter 2001).

More Resources From The Author

BLOG : www.somequietthoughts.blogspot.com

YouVersion Devotionals QR Code

YOU VERSION DEVOTIONALS

- YouVersion plan '**Know, Grow, Show. Reflections From John 15'.**
- YouVersion plan '**Called and Chosen - Understanding Your Identity and Destiny in Christ.**
- YouVersion plan: **The Well Trimmed Wick: Finishing Well and Strong.**
- YouVersion plan: **The Continuum: Rooted, Built Up & Strengthened.**
- YouVersion plan: **Hope: The Kind That Keeps Us Going.**
- YouVersion plan: **Creating a Counter Culture - a Study on the**

Beatitudes.
- YouVersion plan: **Come to the Table.**
- YourVersion Plan: **The Future Will Write Your History.**
- YouVersion plan: **Peace on Earth.**
- YouVersion plan: **Idols of the Heart.**
- YouVersion plan: **Two Bookends: The Fear of the Lord and Being Kept in His Love**
- YouVersion plan: **The Love of God - the Plumbline**
- YouVersion plan: **Temptation: Why can't I say no?**

Know Grow Show : A Reflection on John 15, by Navaz D'Cruz is also available in Amazon, Flipkart and Kindle. Please scan the QR code to purchase a copy.

www.ingramcontent.com/pod-product-compliance
Lightning Source LLC
Chambersburg PA
CBHW041324120726
48005CB00014B/2113